LONDON PORN

MAGNUS BECKMAN

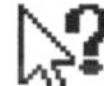

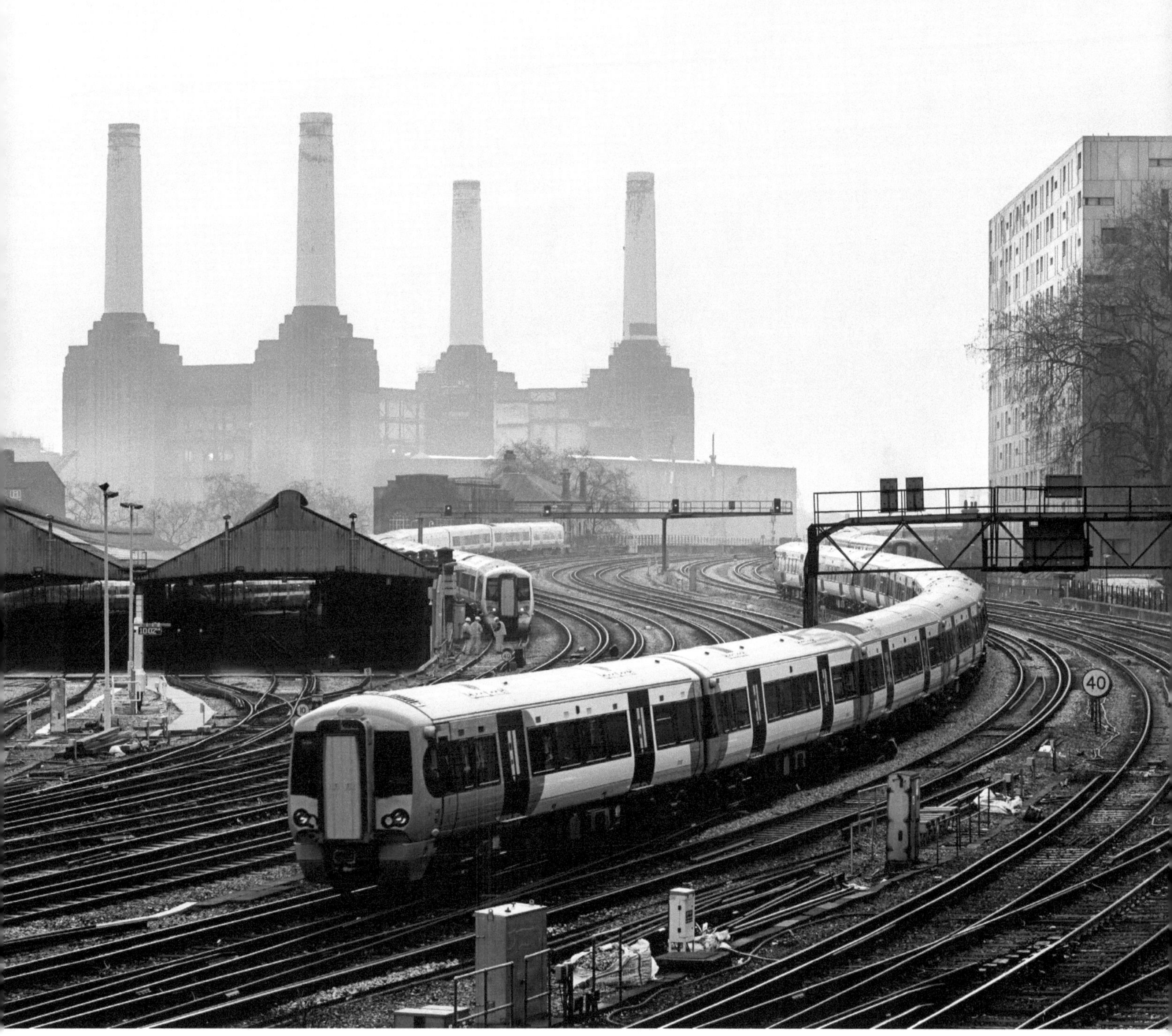

Photo by Andres Garcia

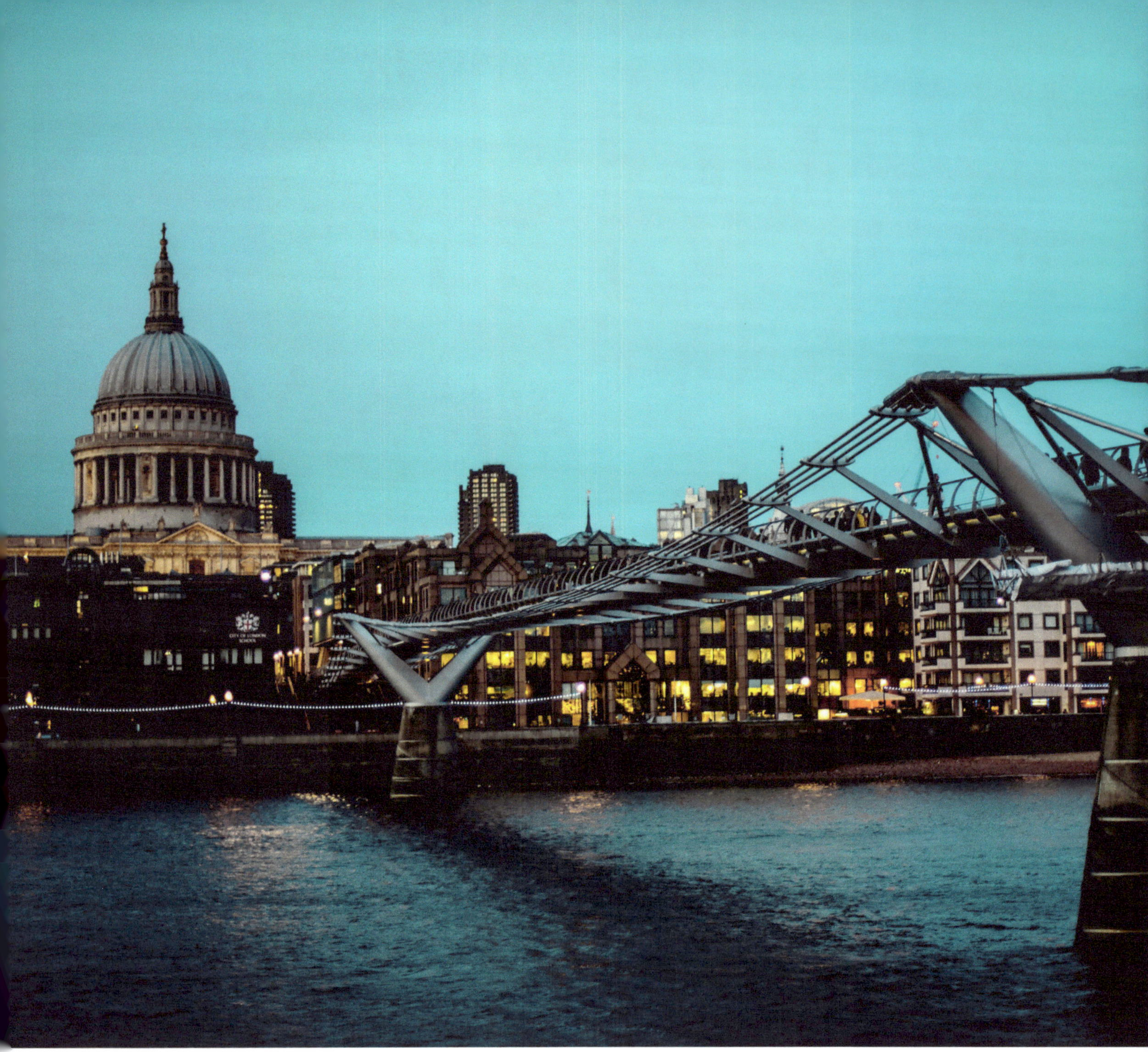

Photo by Anthony Delanoix

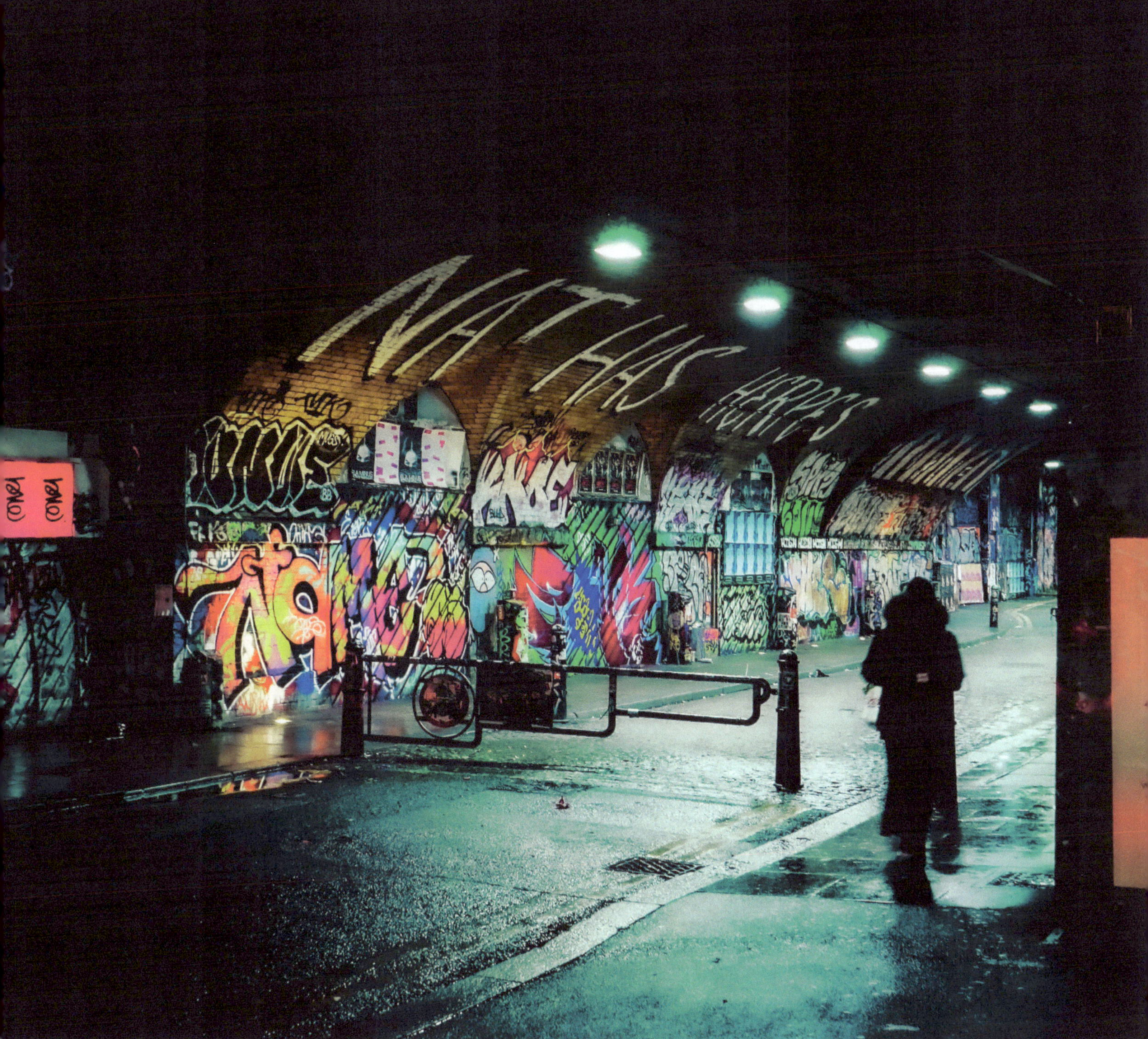

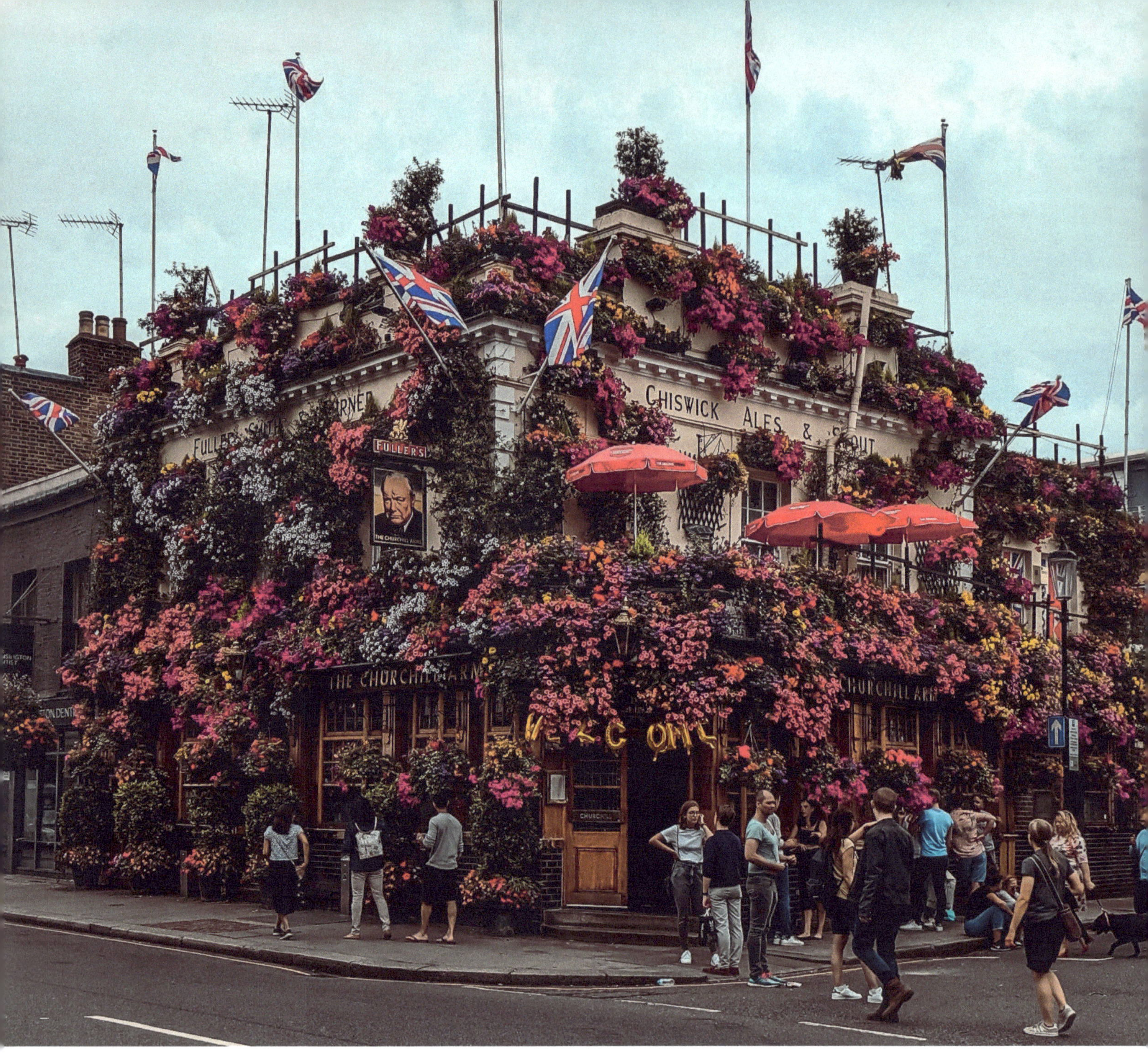

Photo by Alex Motoc

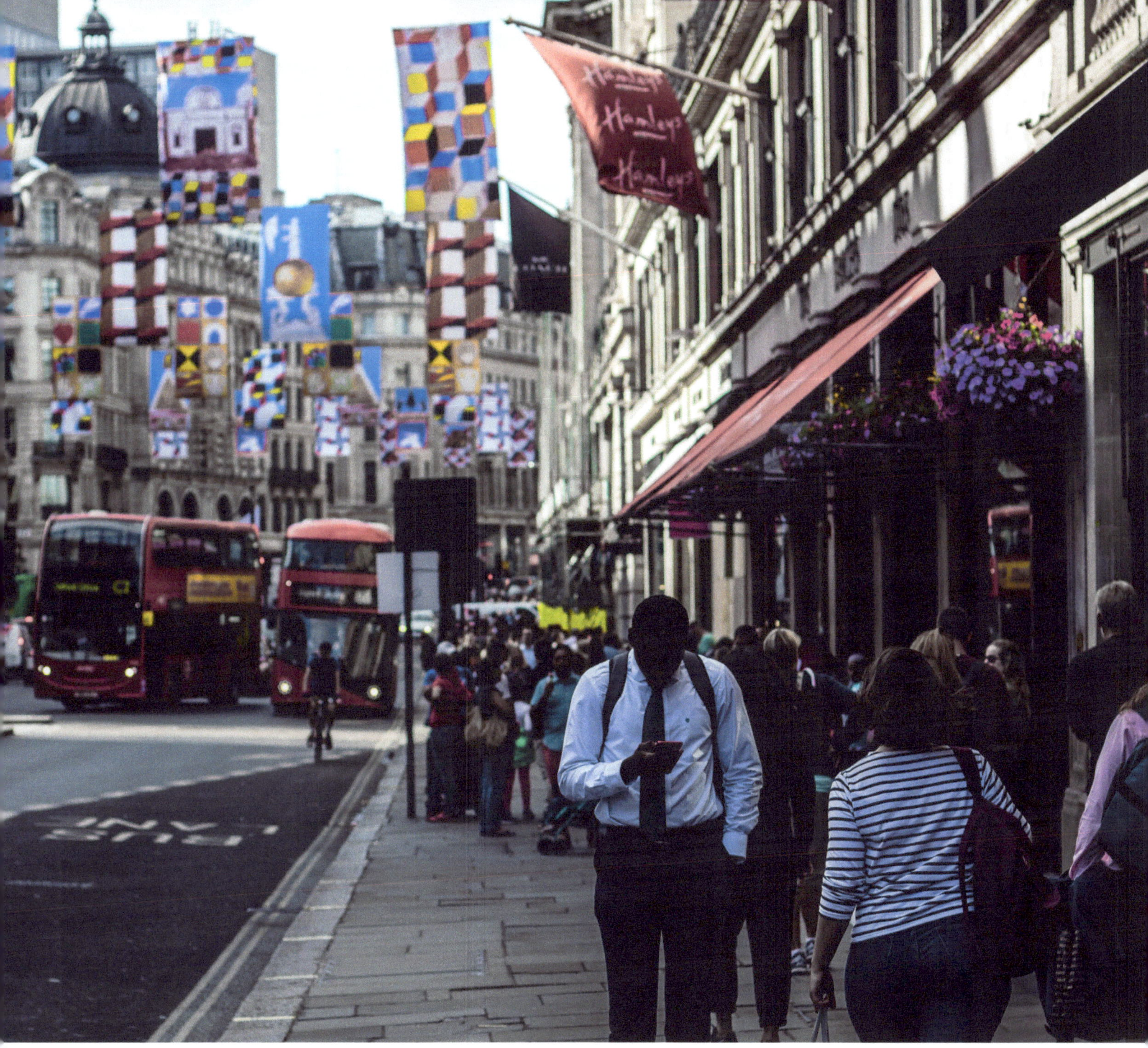

Photo by Arthur Edelman

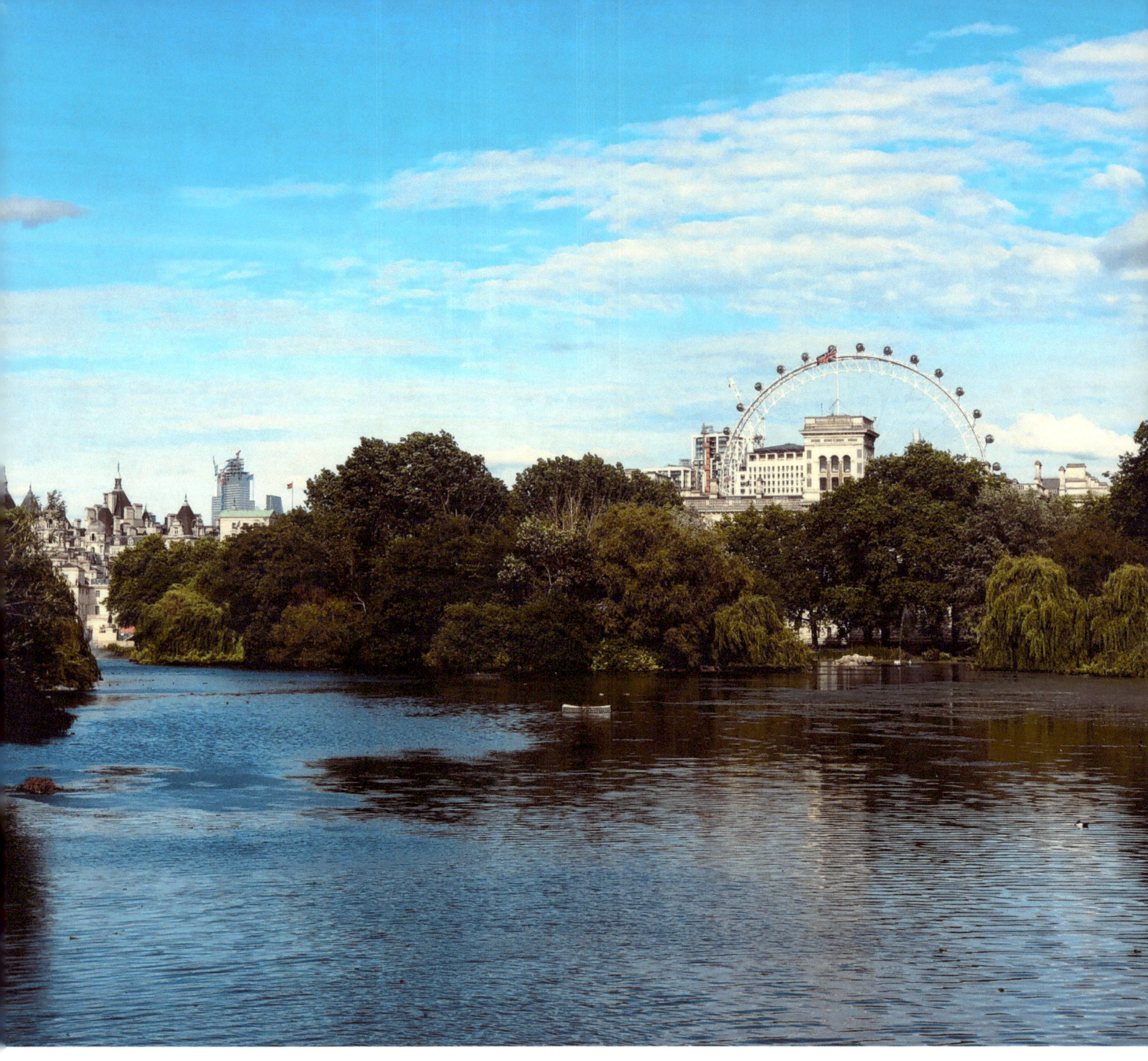

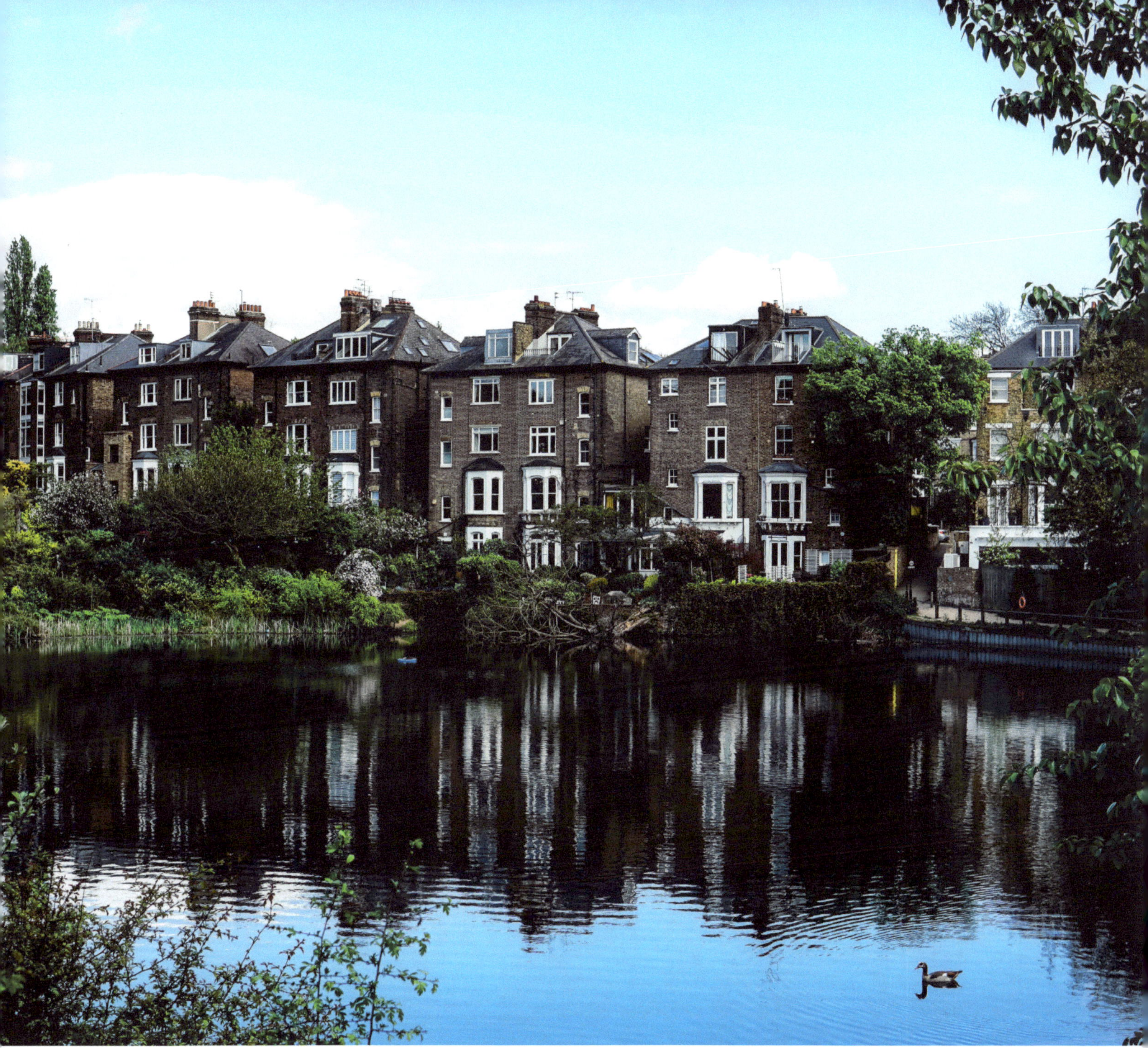

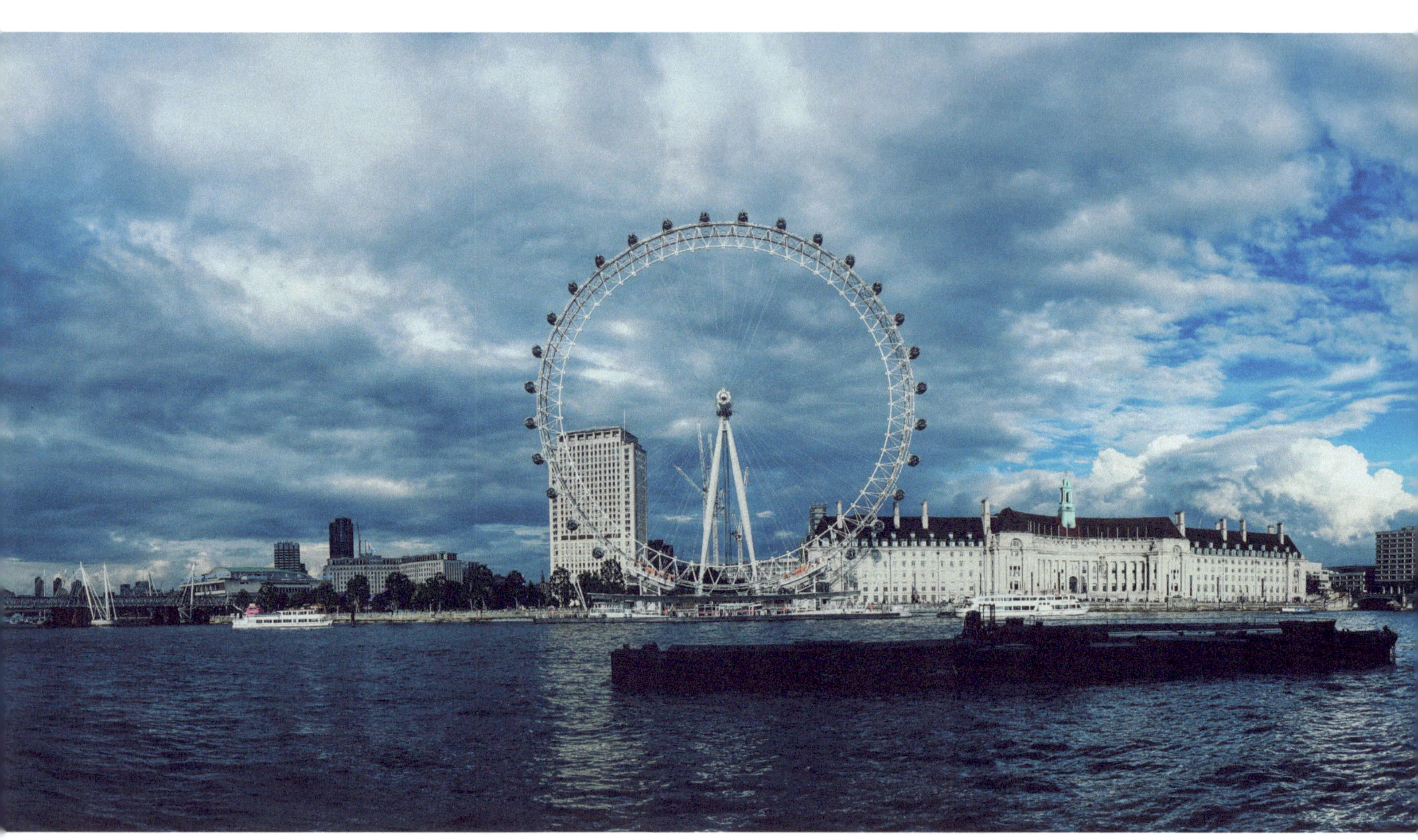

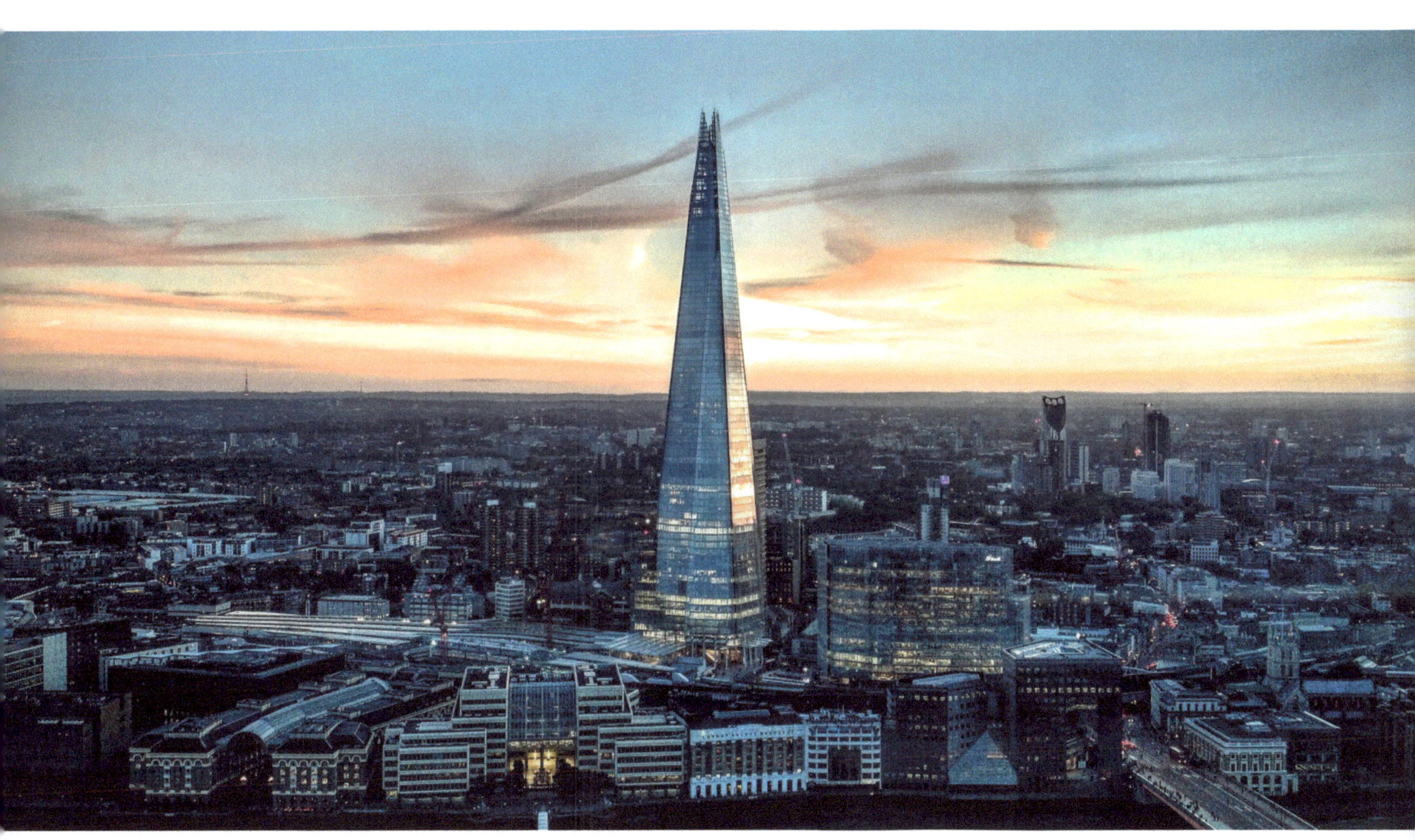

Photo by Fred Moon

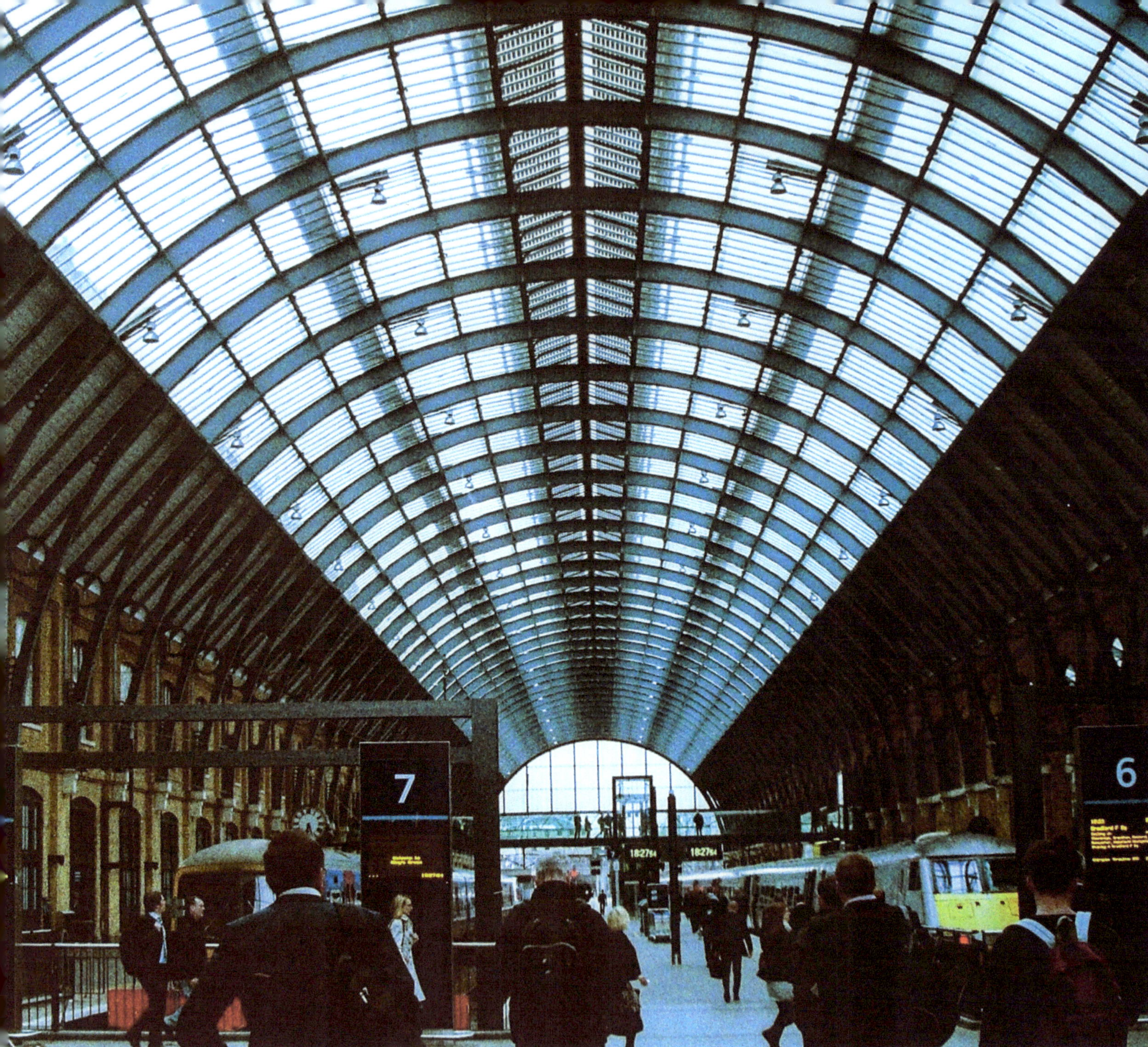

Photo by BDS Photo

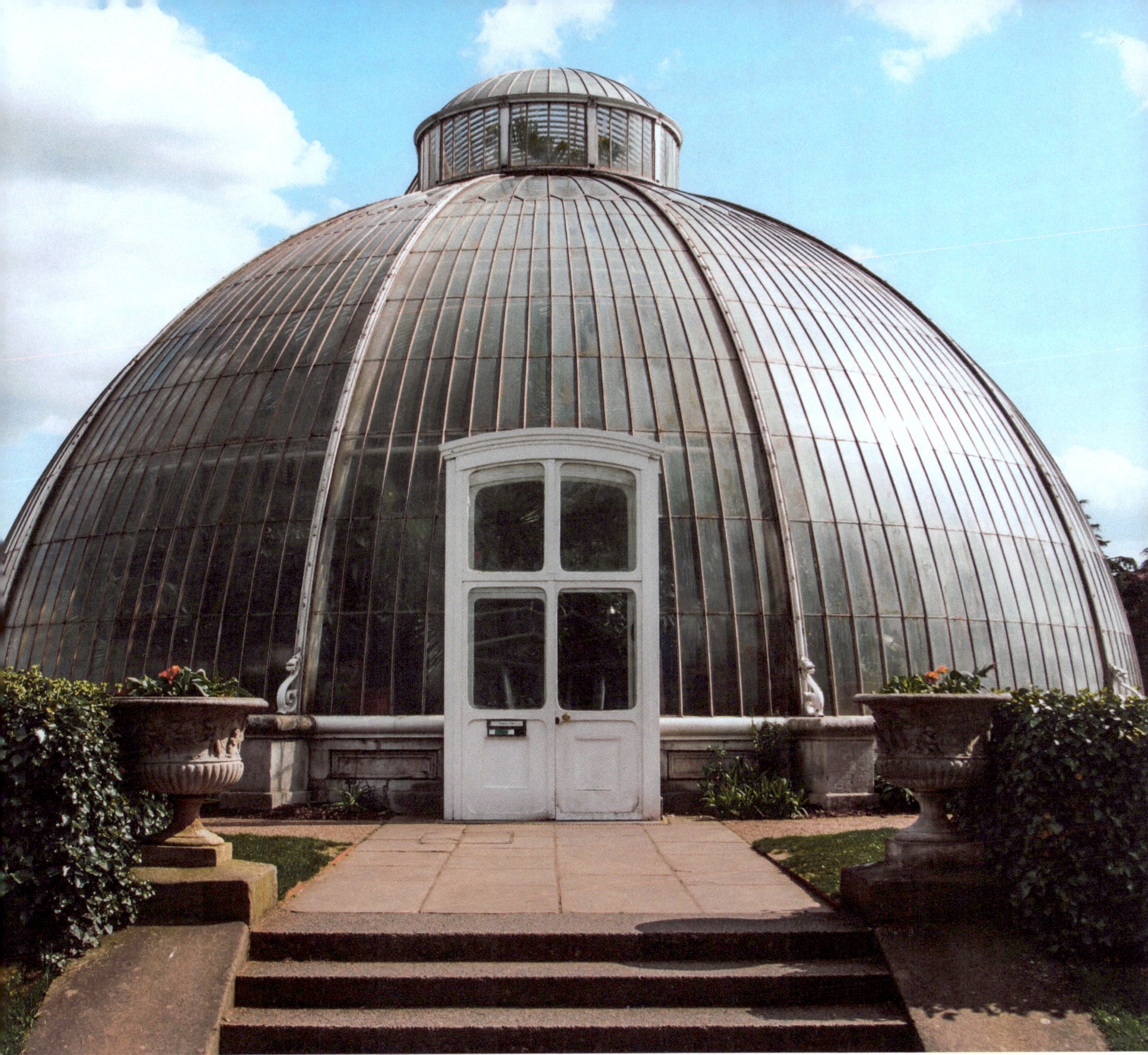

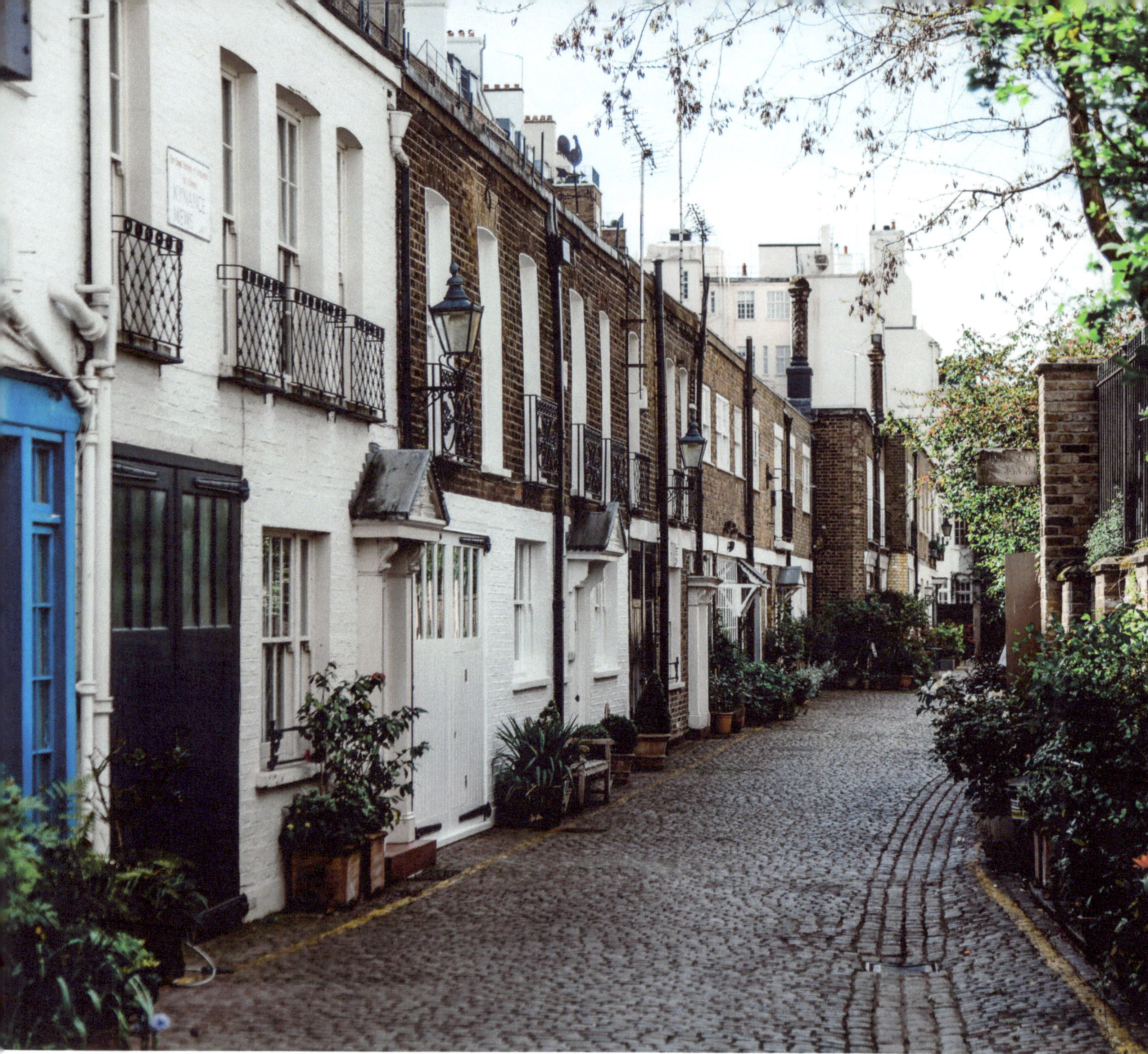

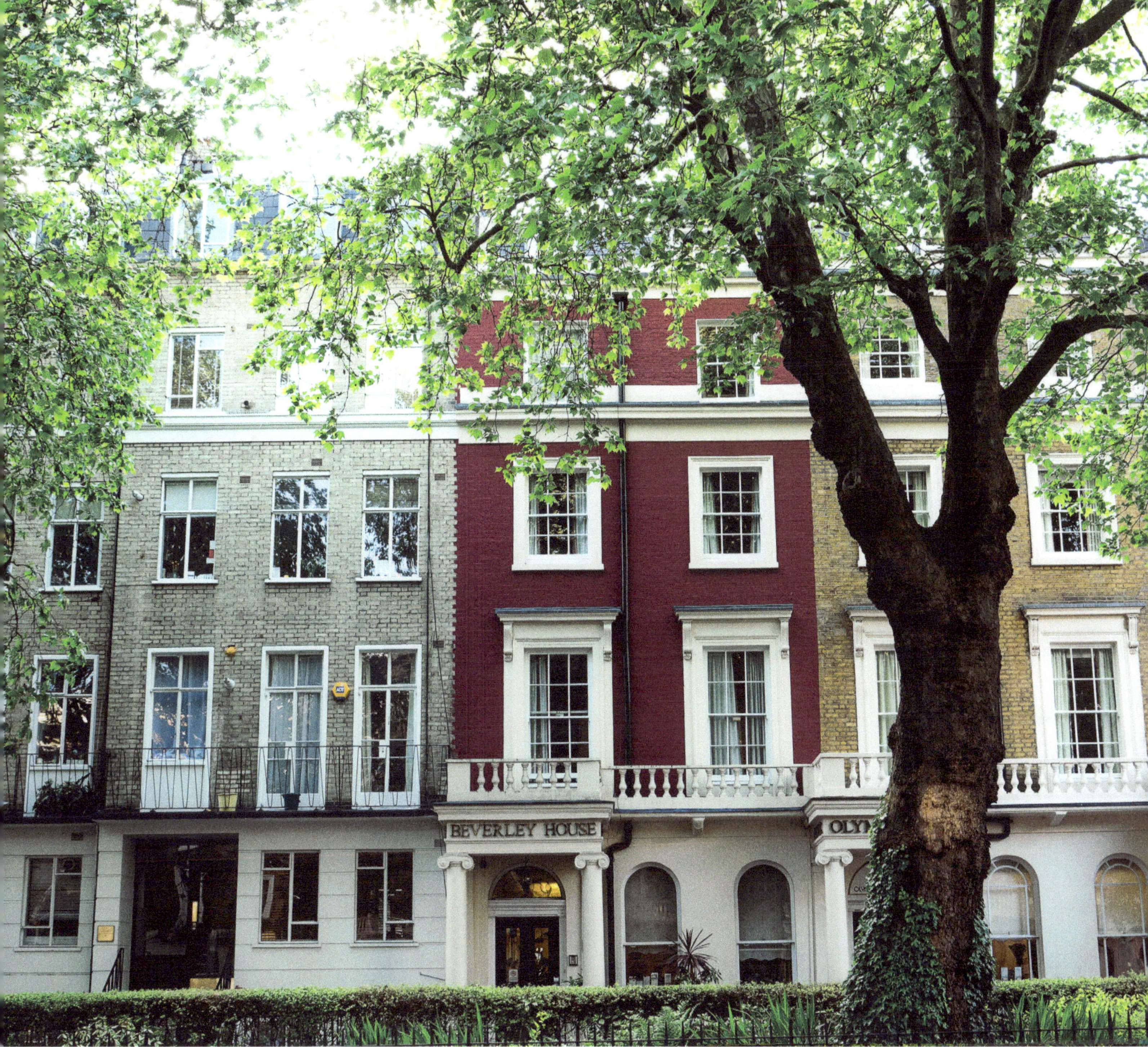

Photo by Camille Brodard

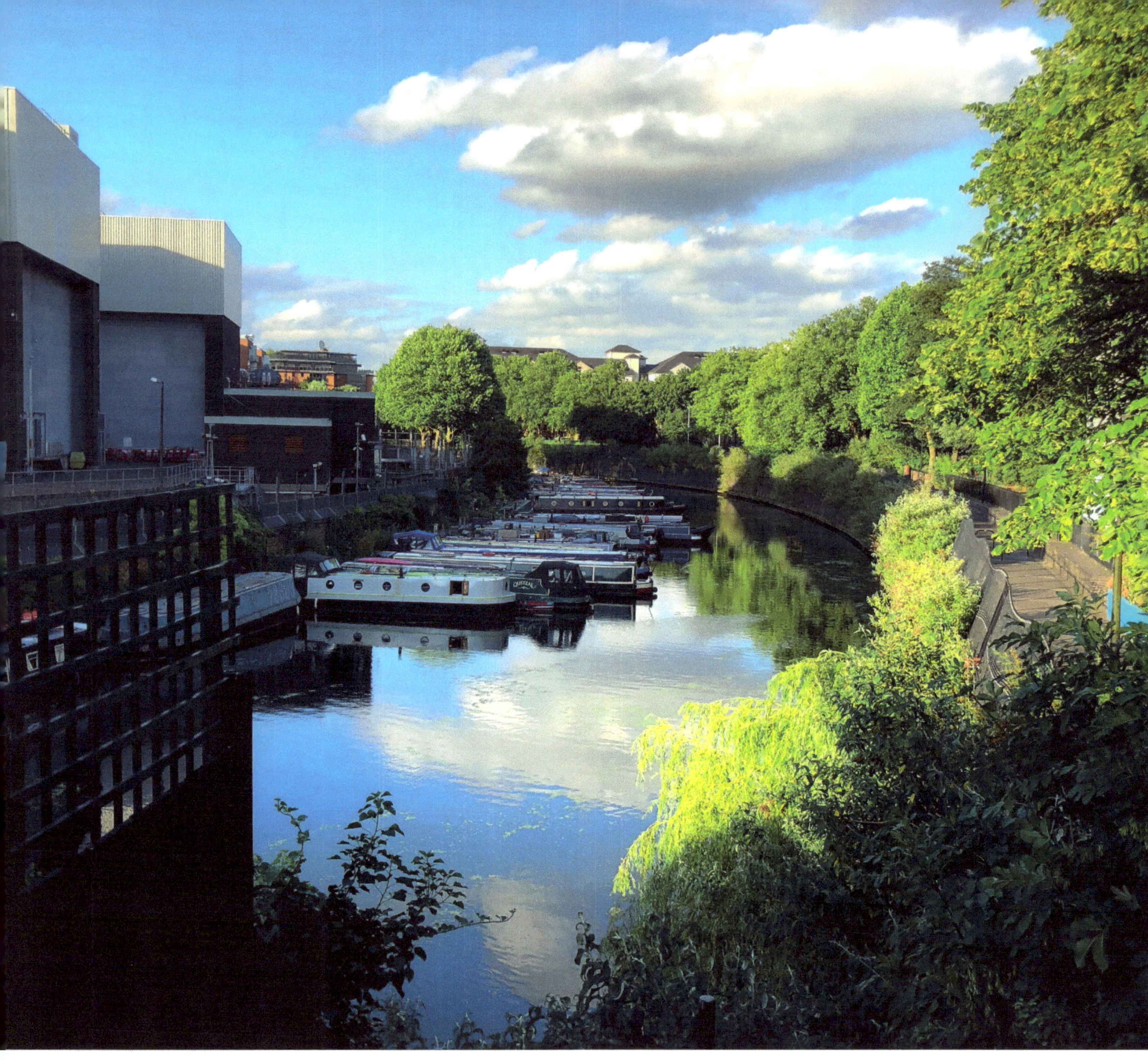

Photo by Dan Poulton

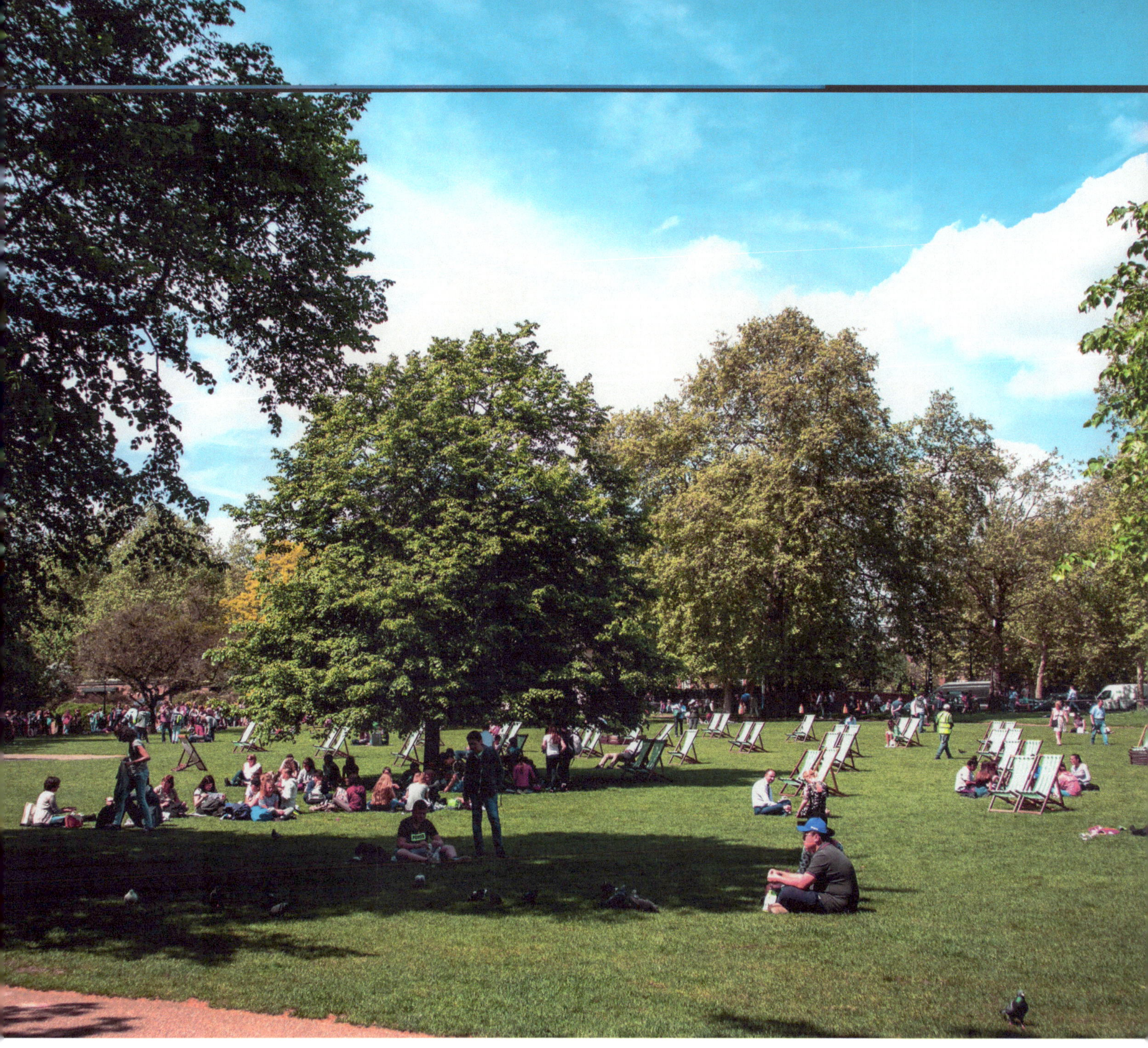

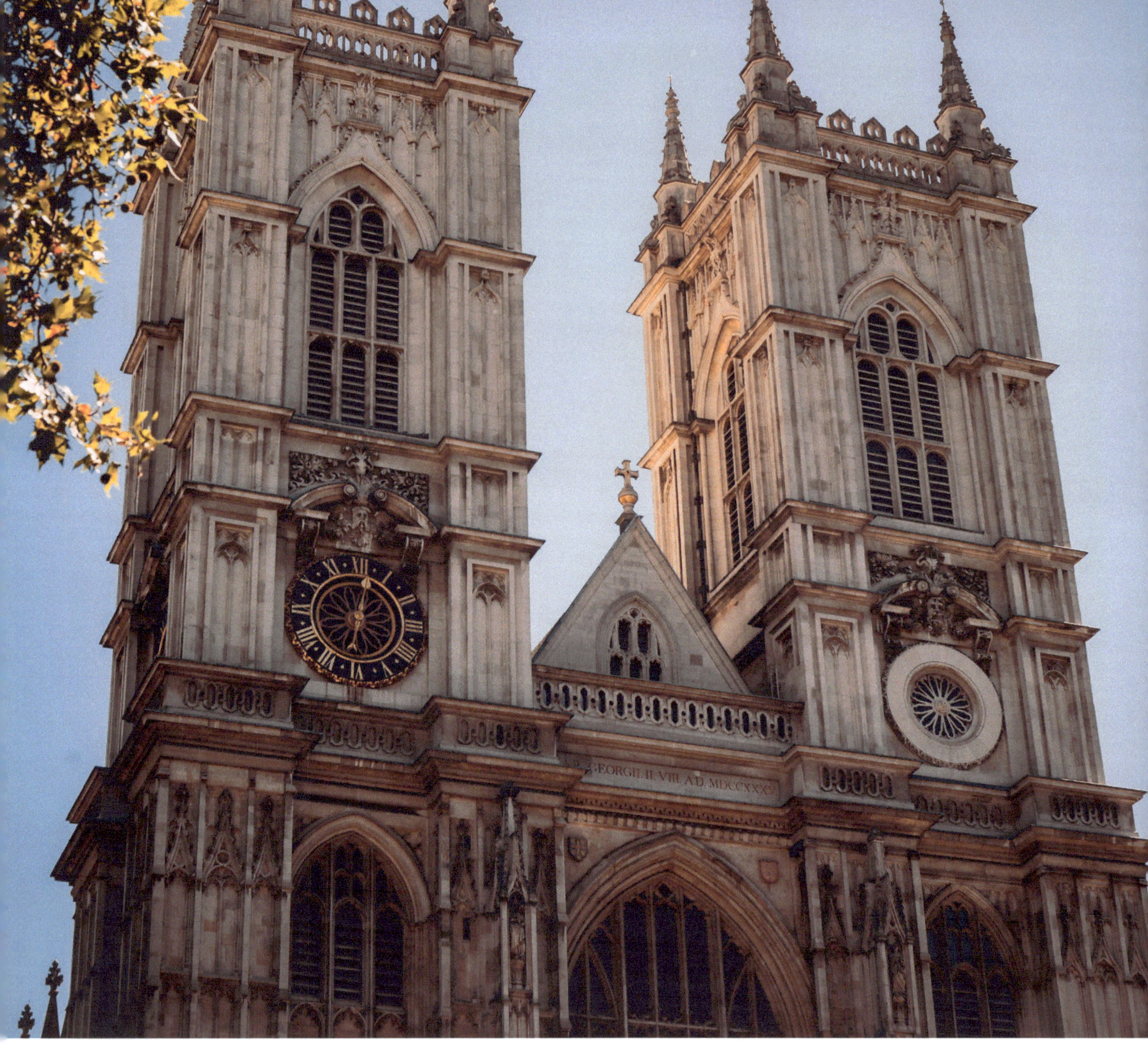

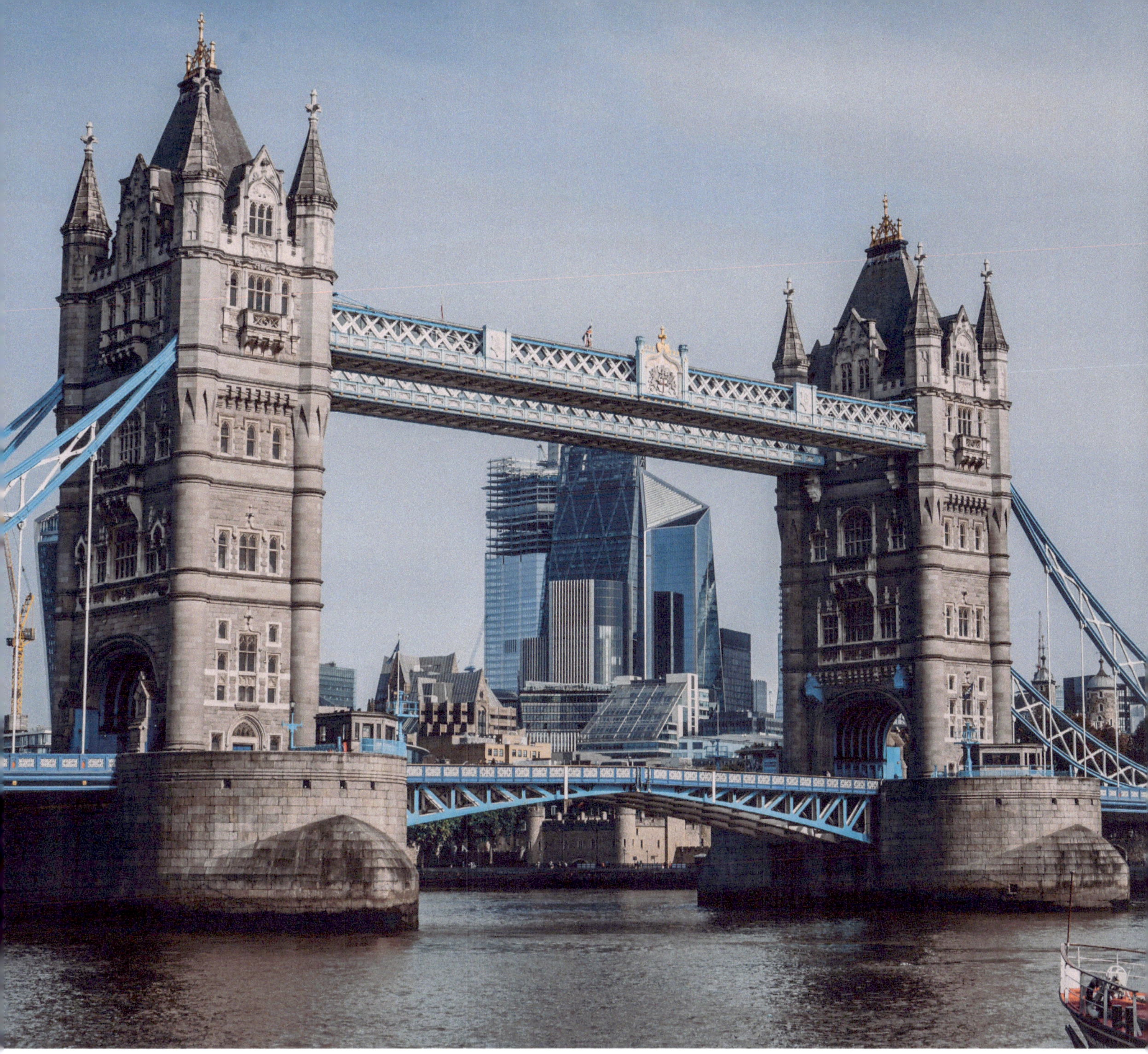

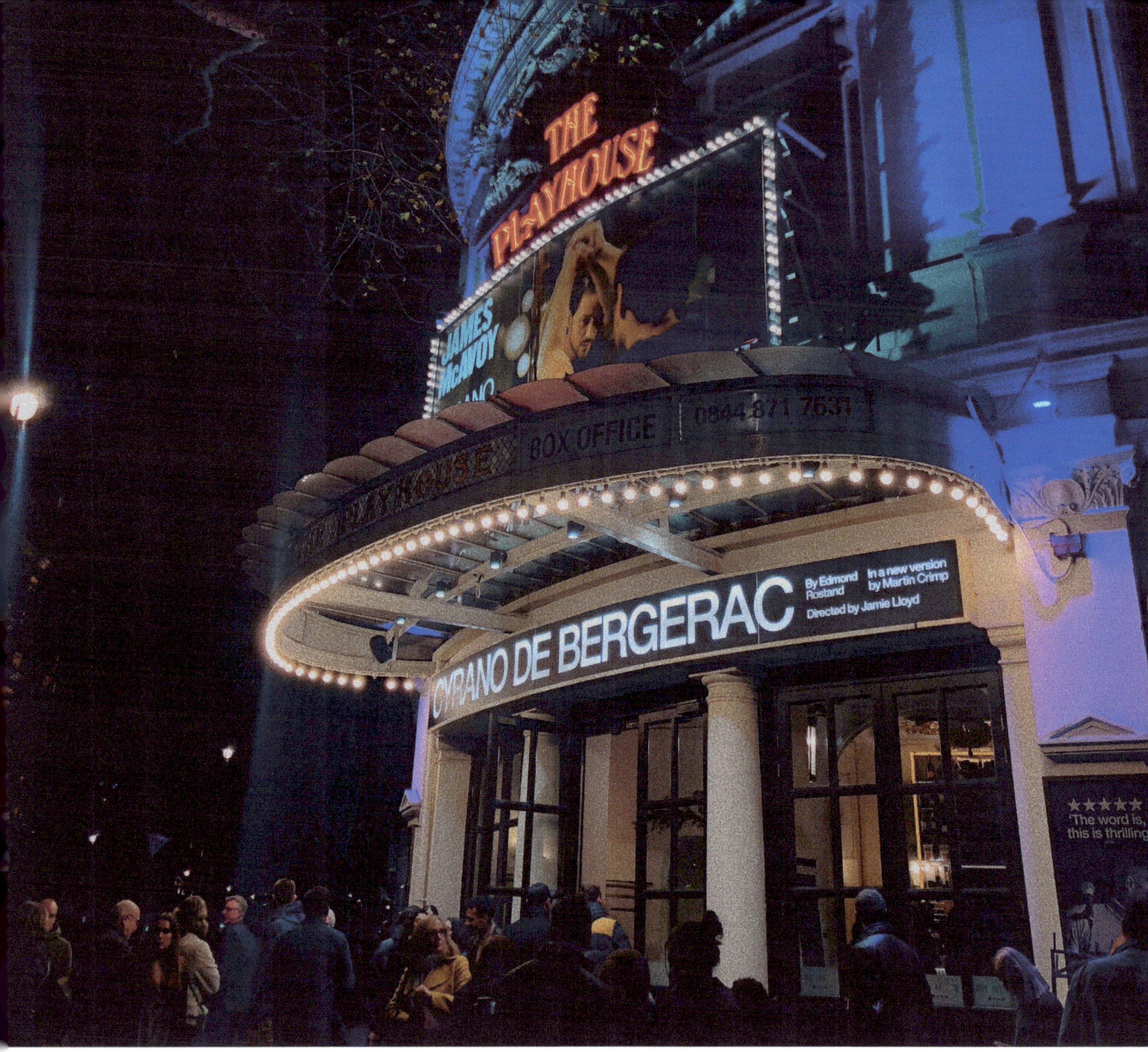

Photo by Darya Tokareva

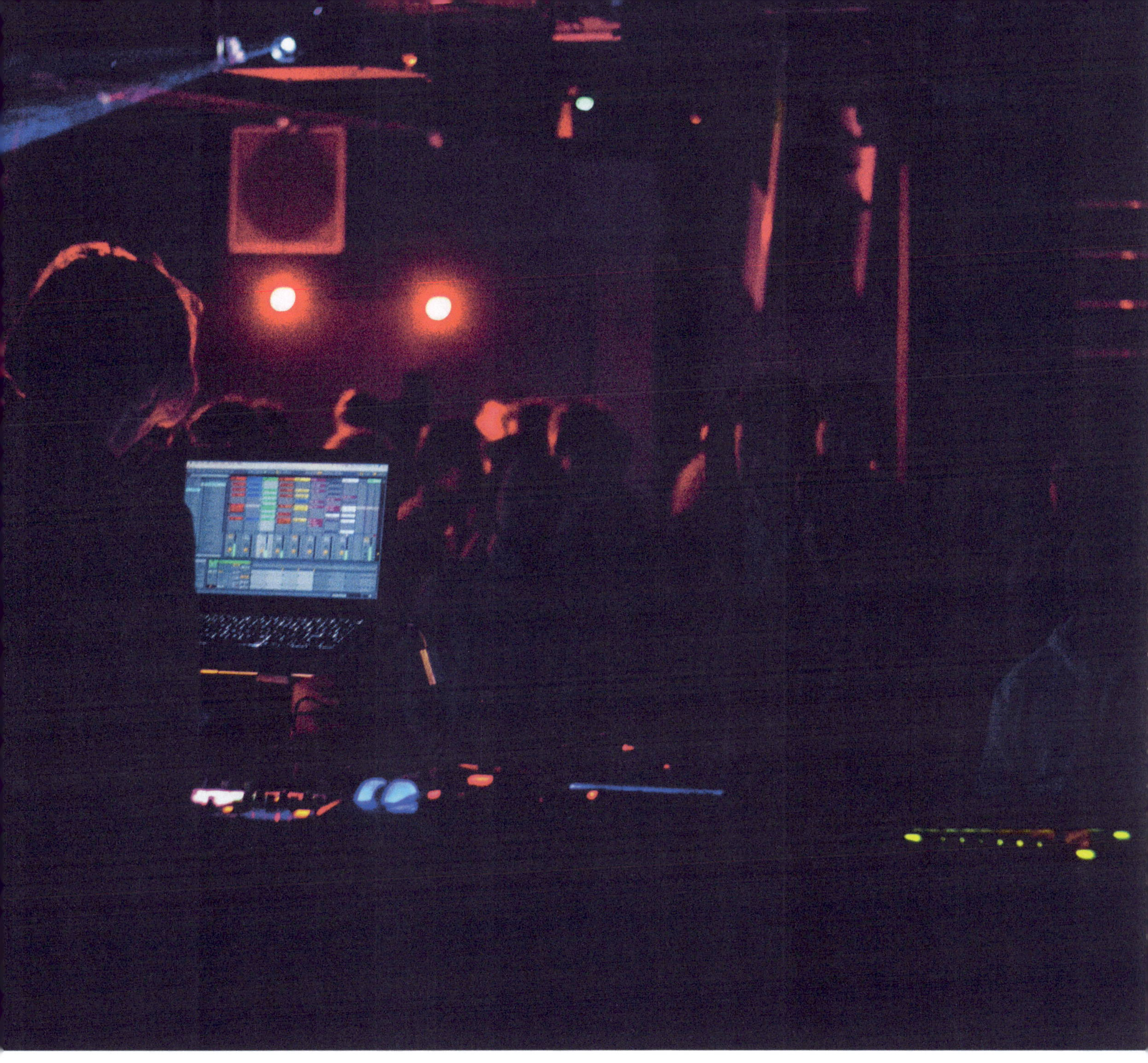

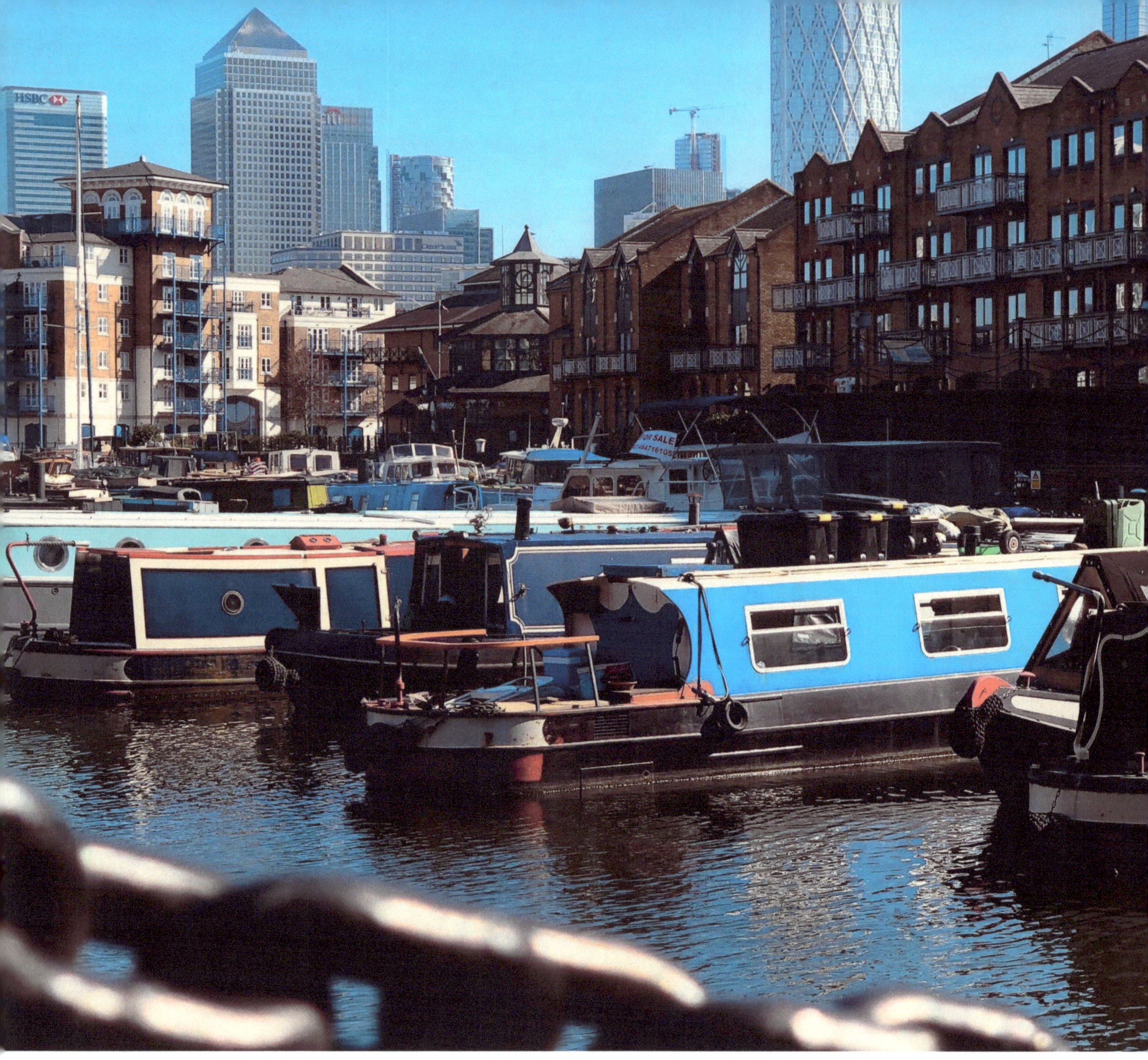

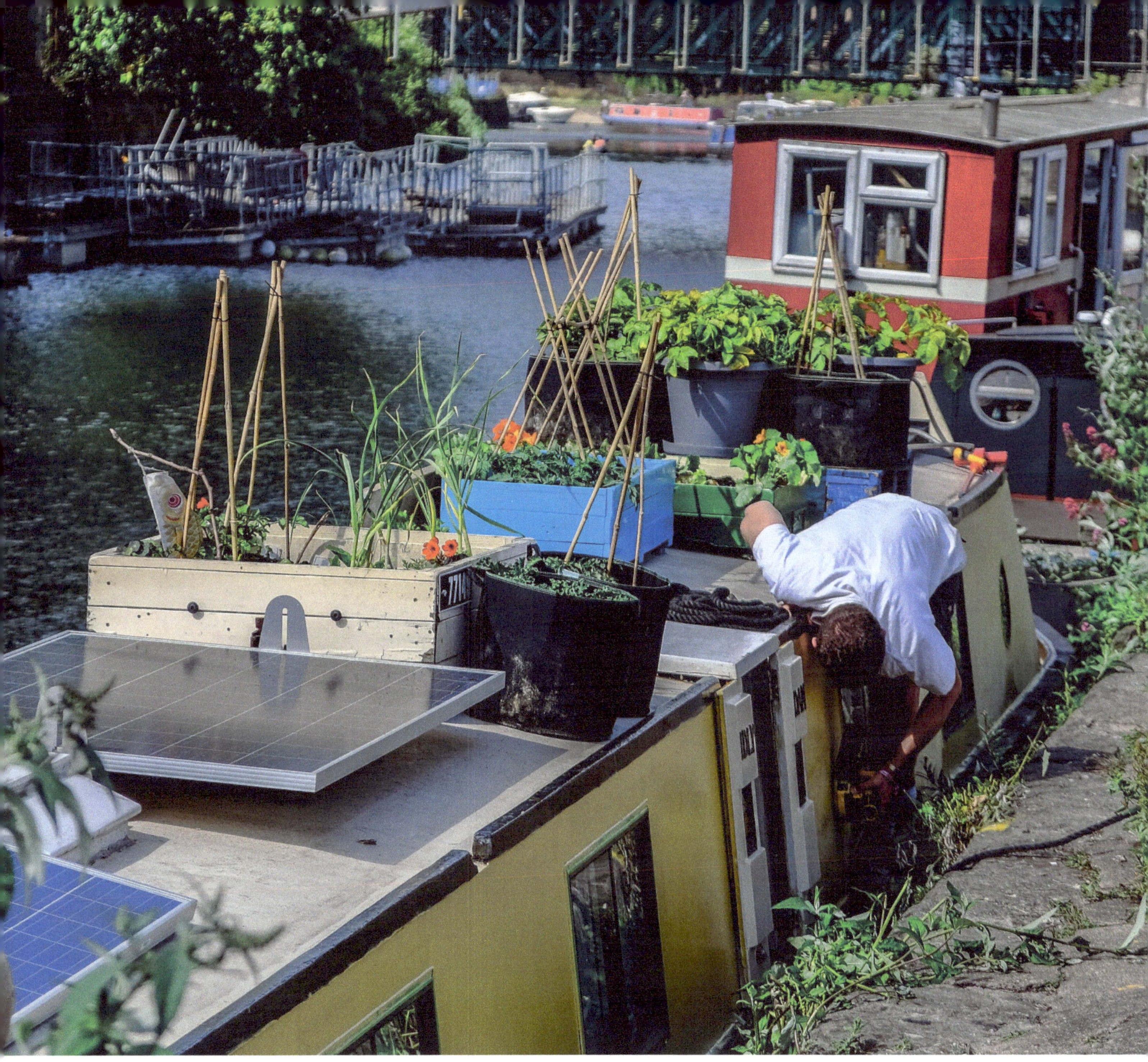

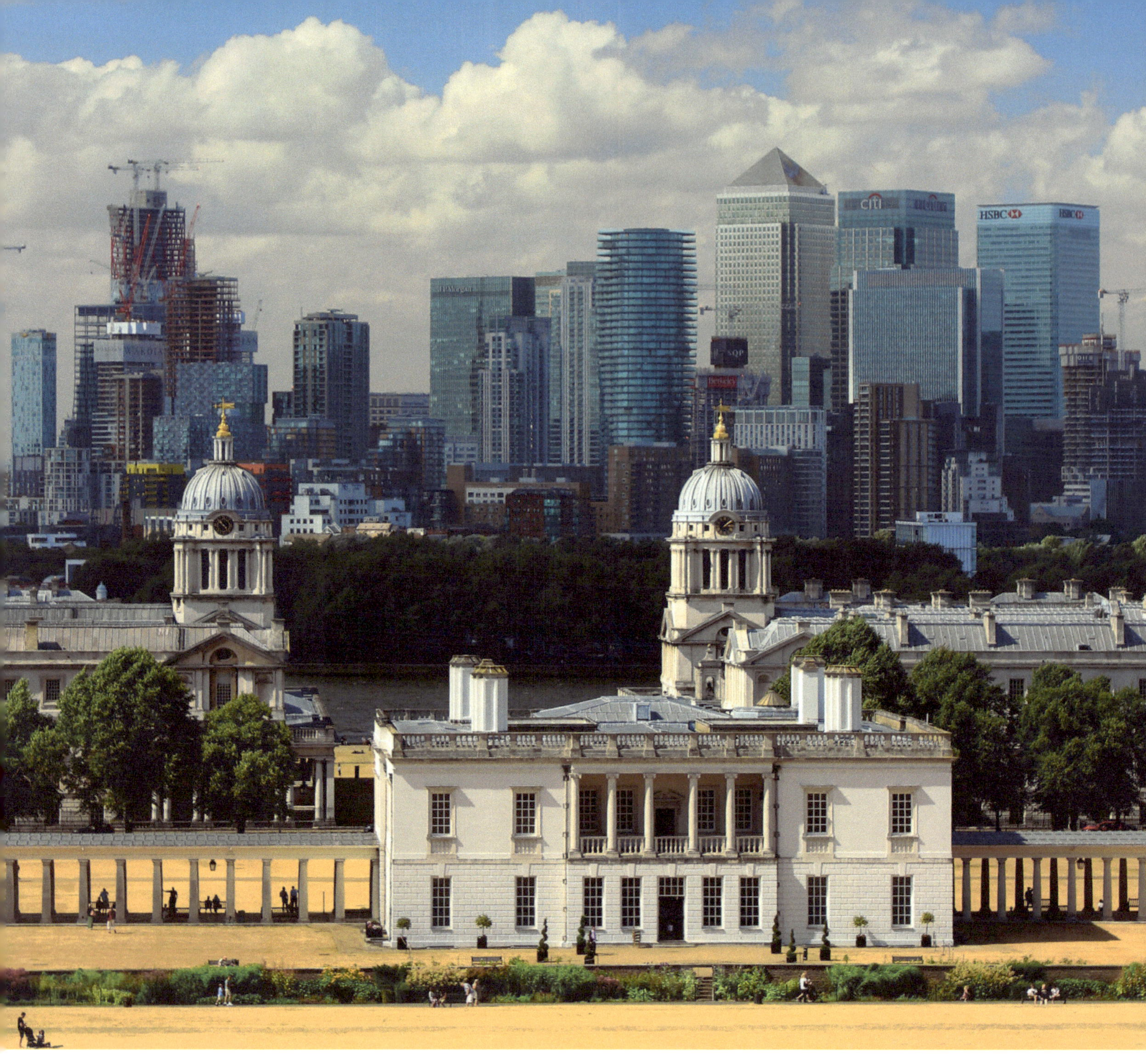

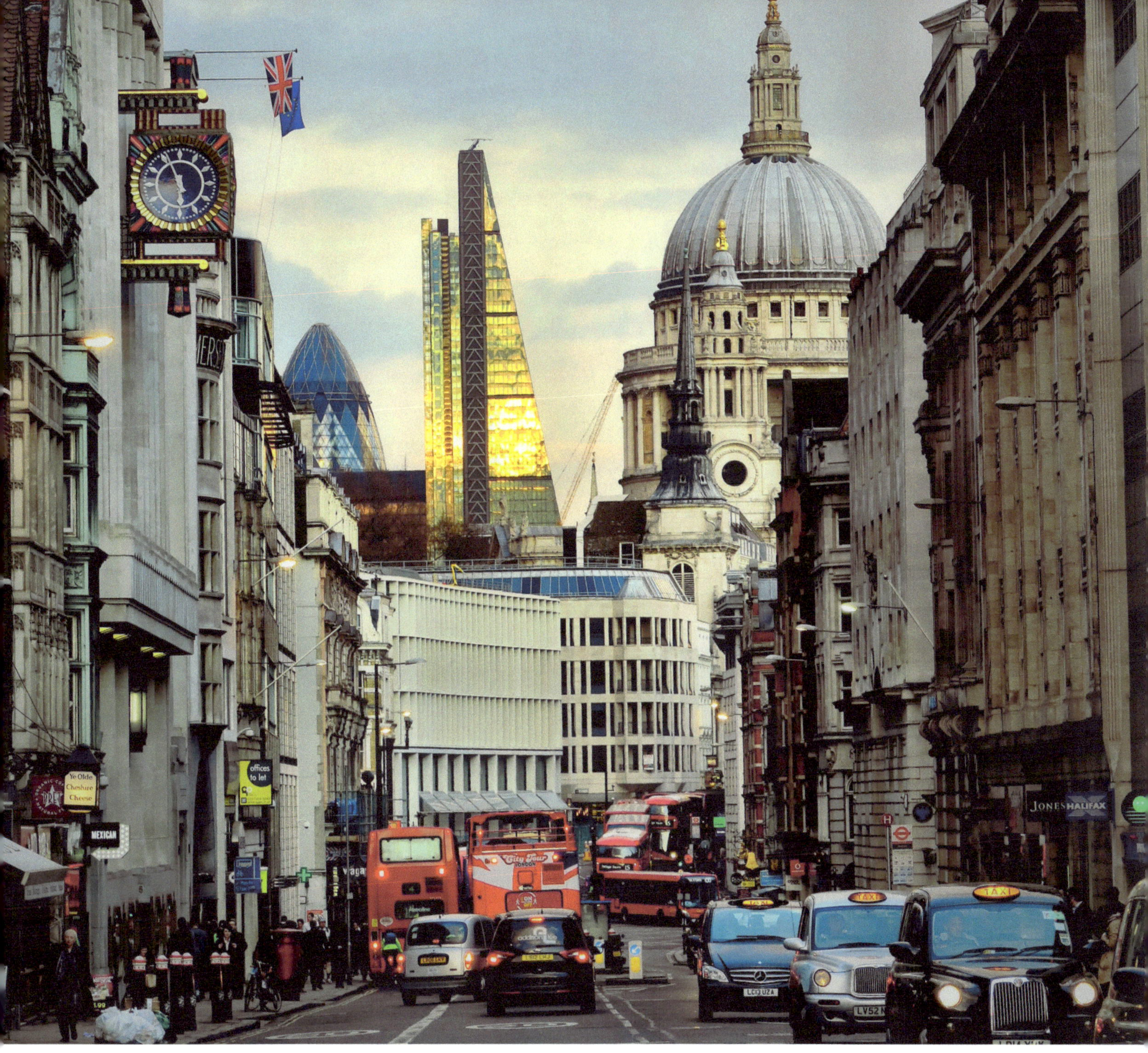

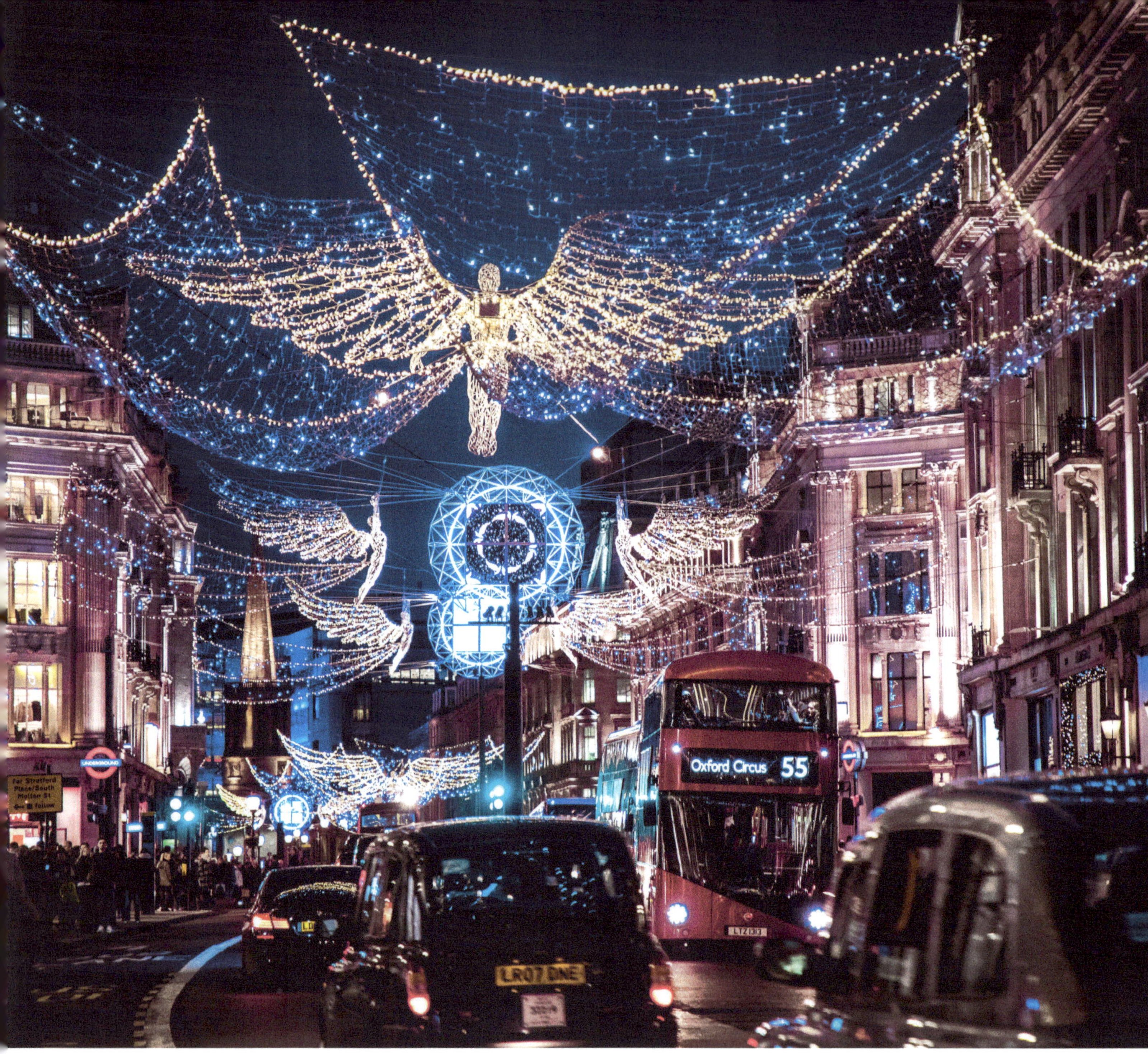

Photo by Jamie Davies

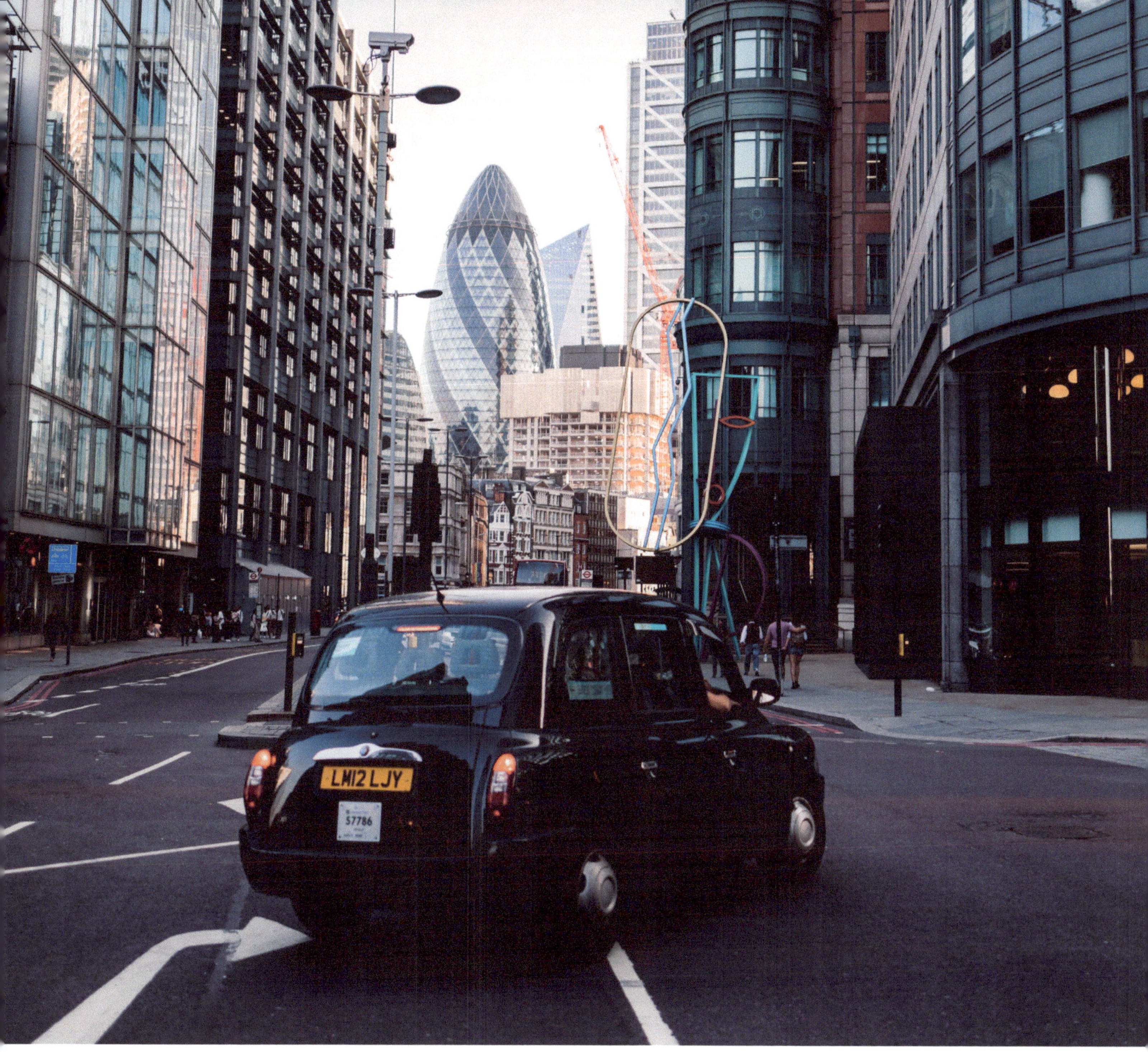

Photo by Humphrey Mule

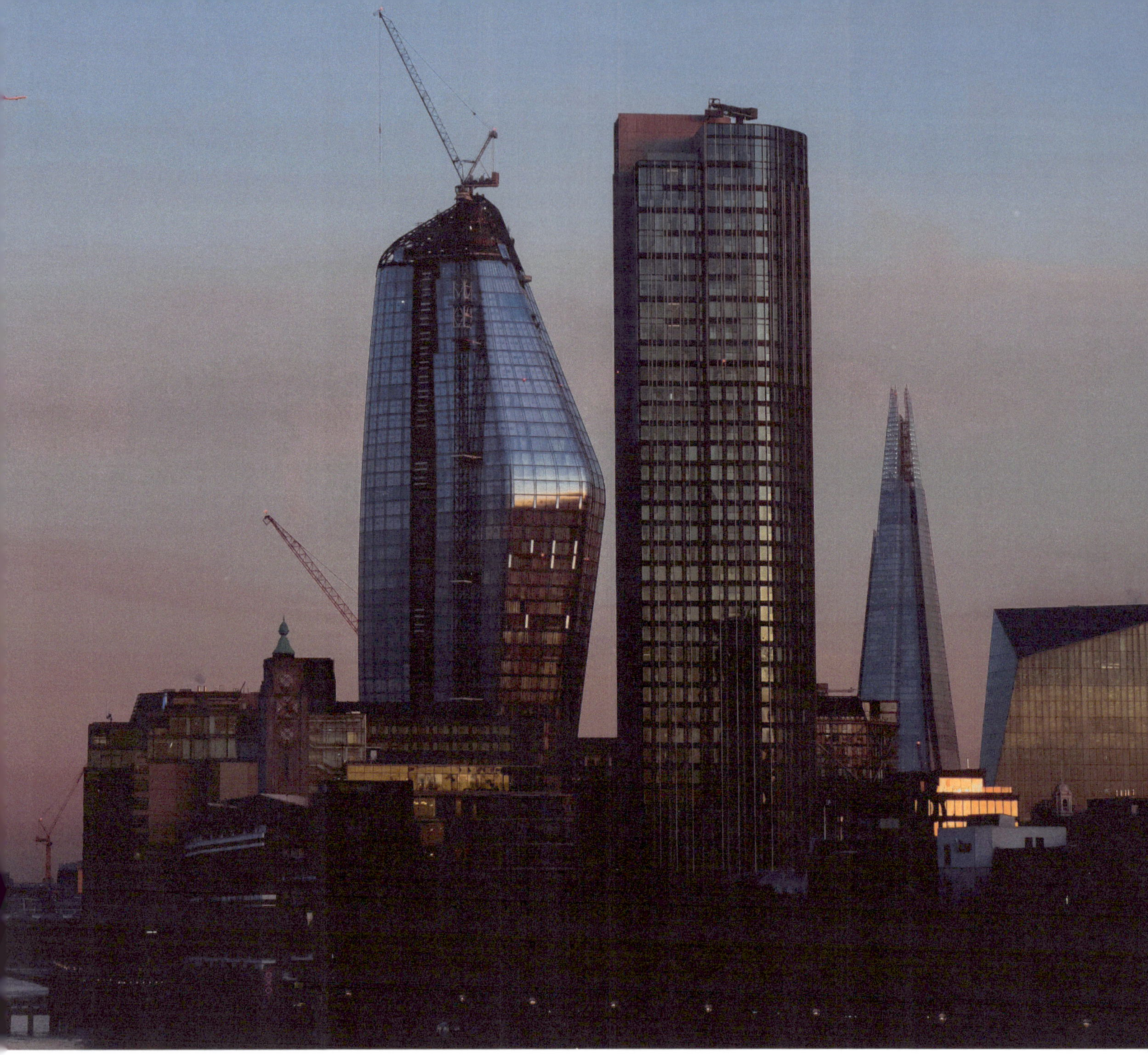

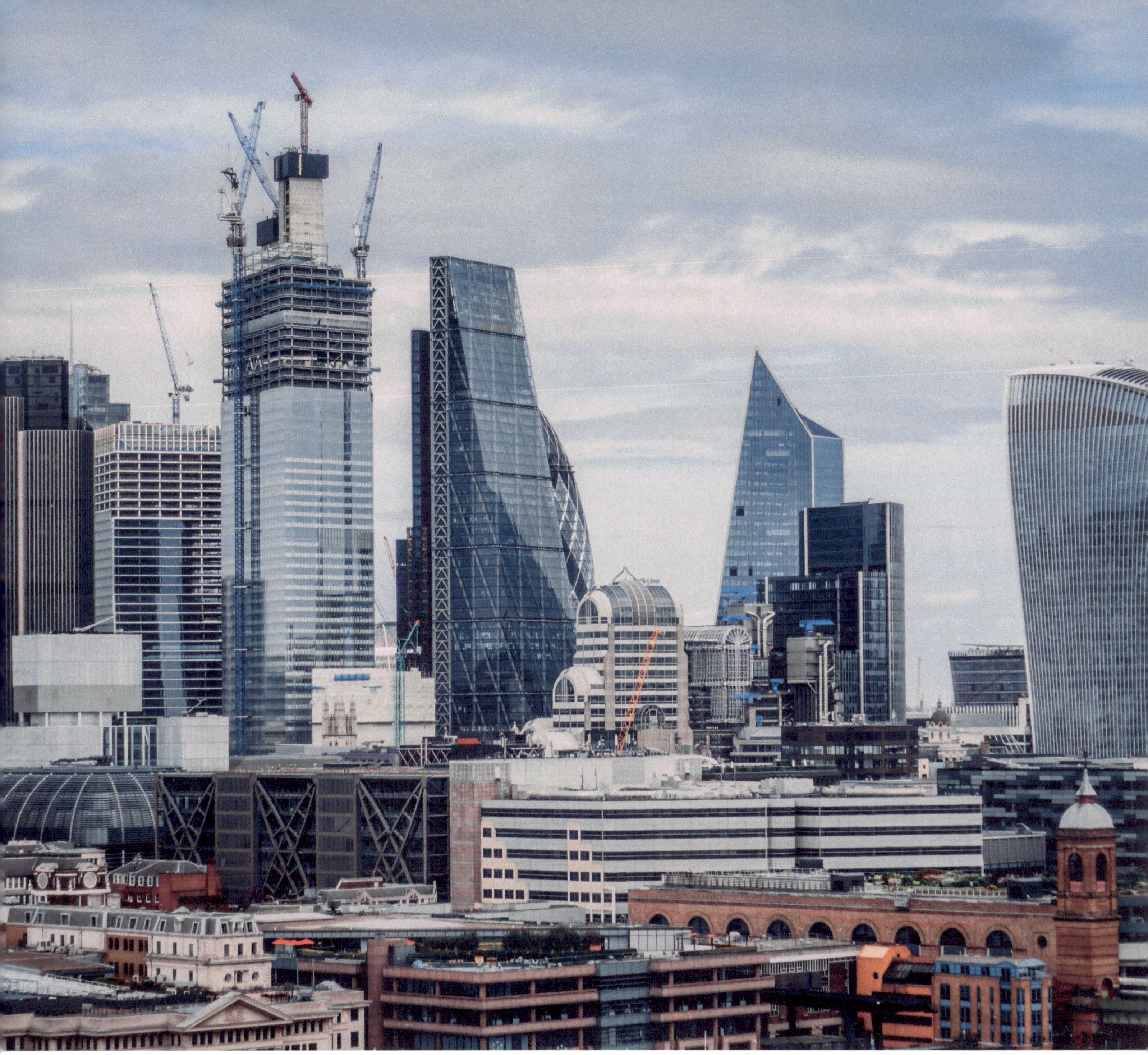

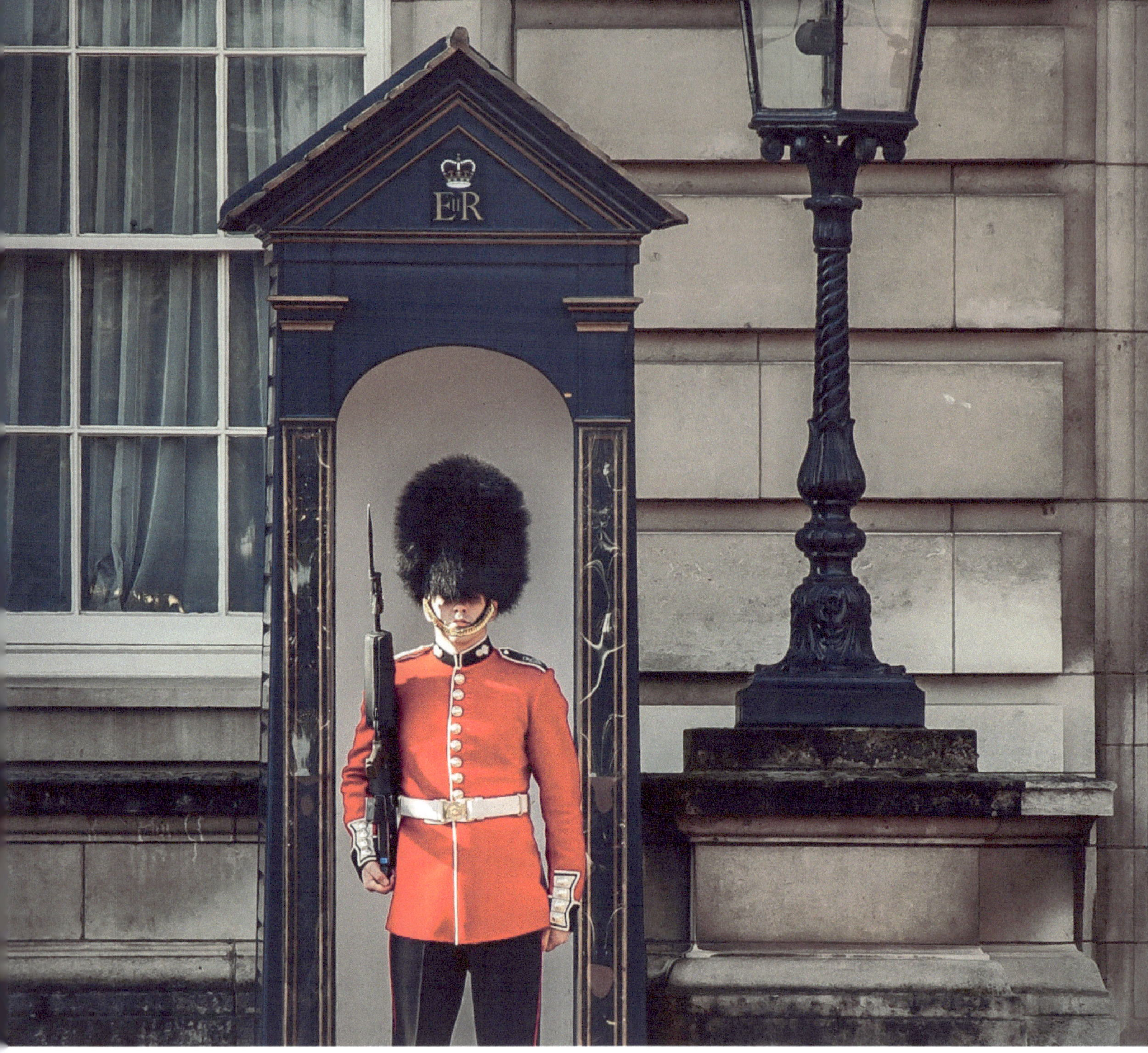

Photo by JJ Ying

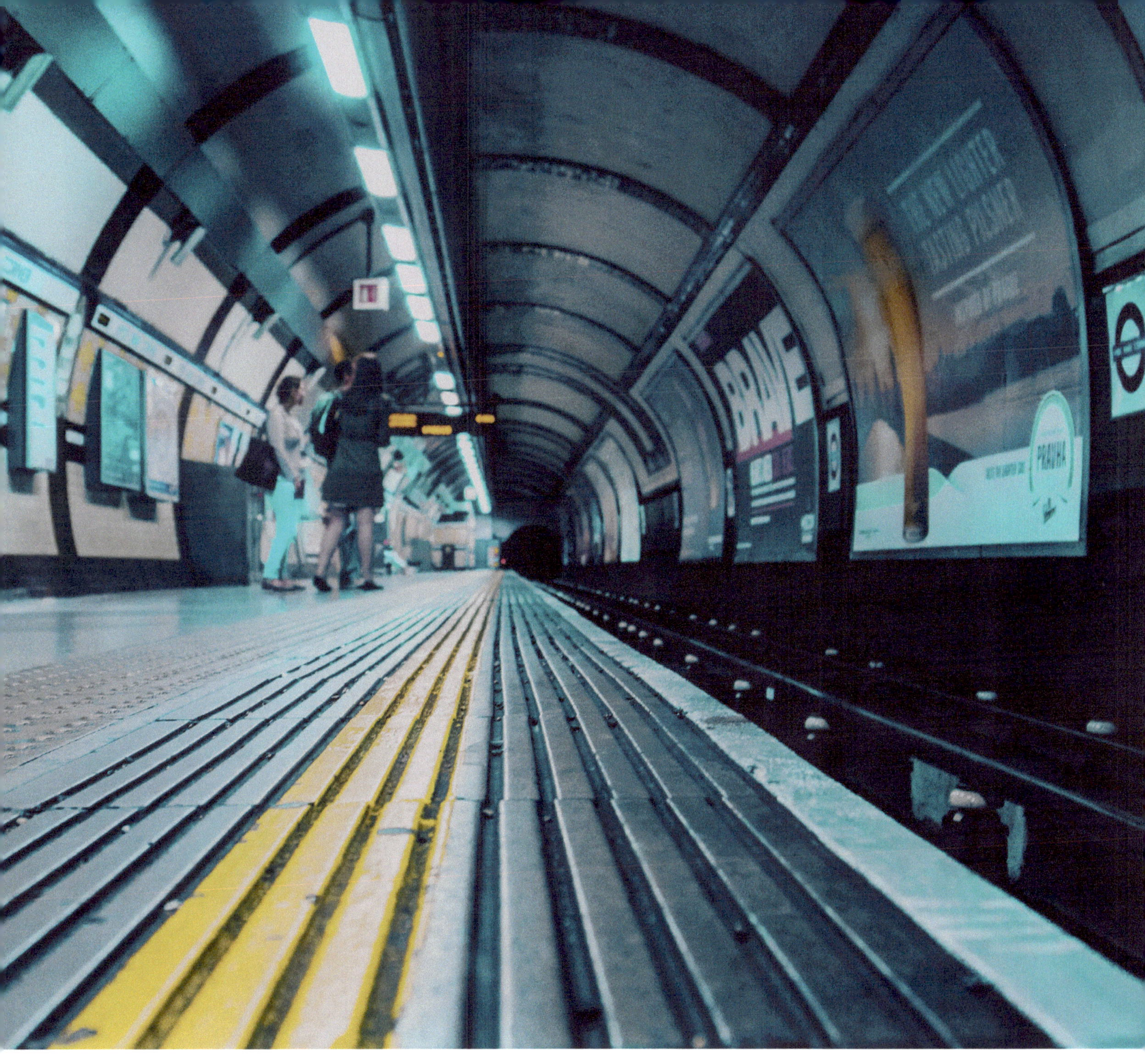

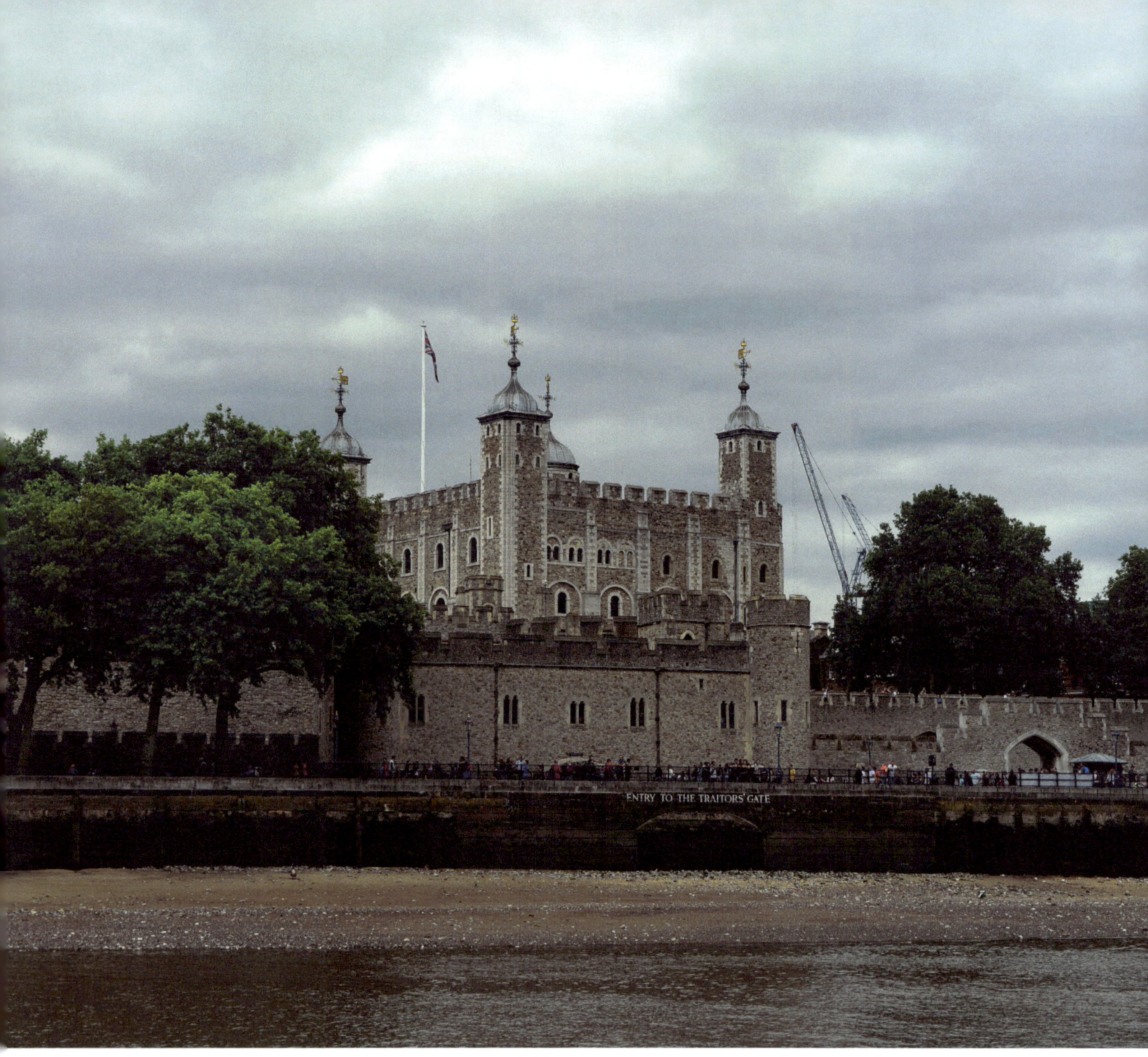

Photo by Joseph Gilbey

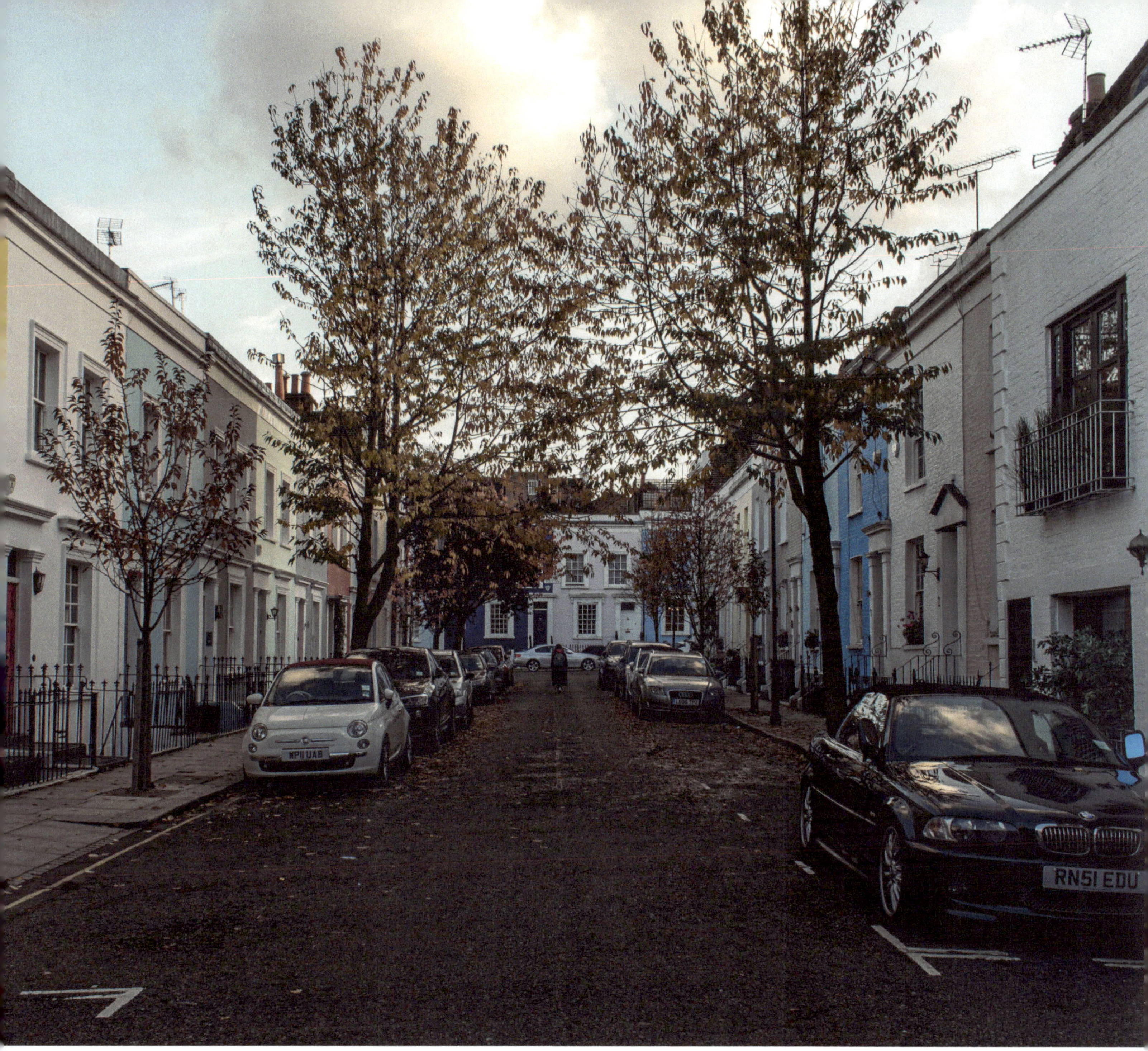

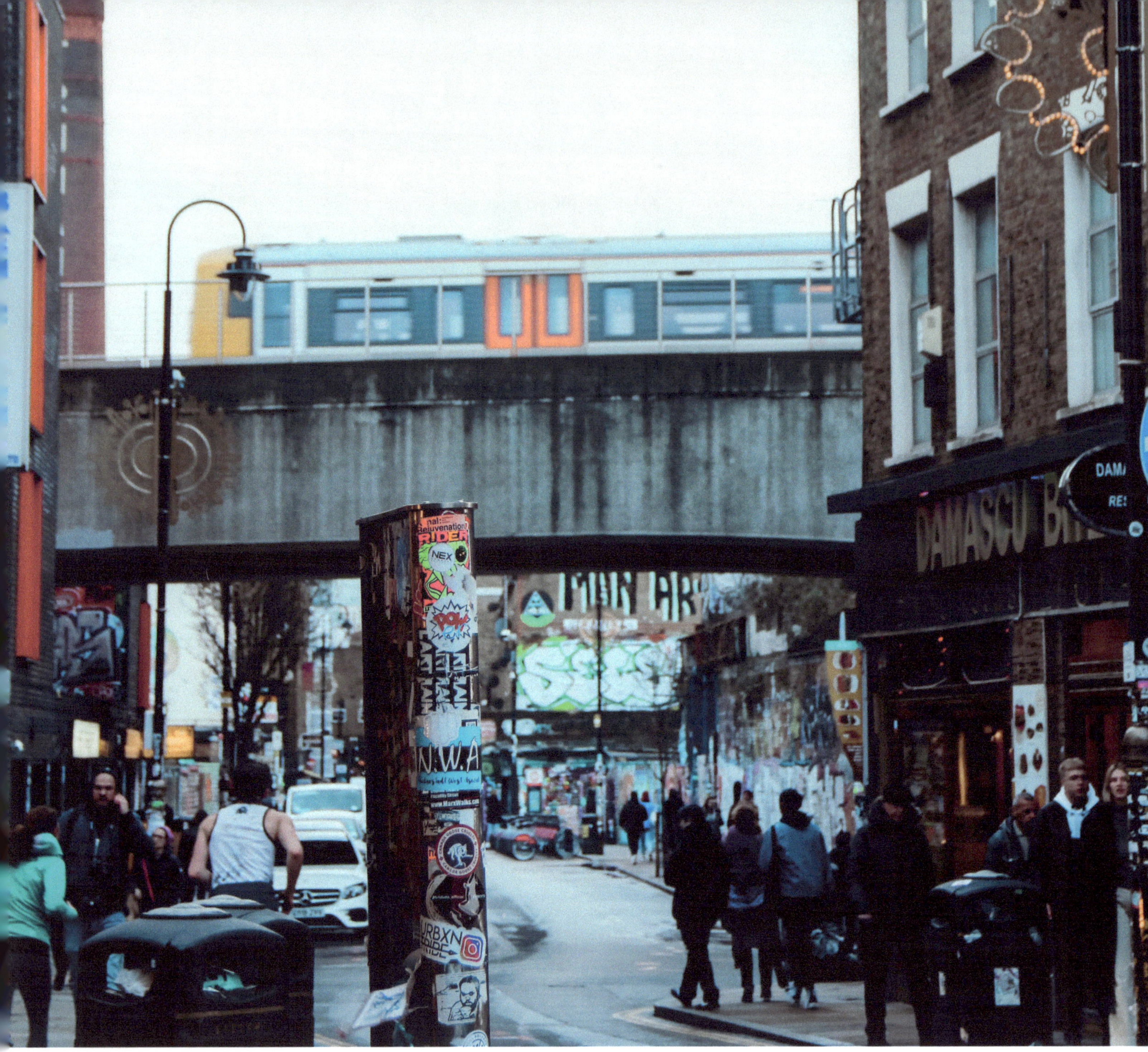

Photo by Leonor Oom

1ºFOºT
CAMDEN LOCK

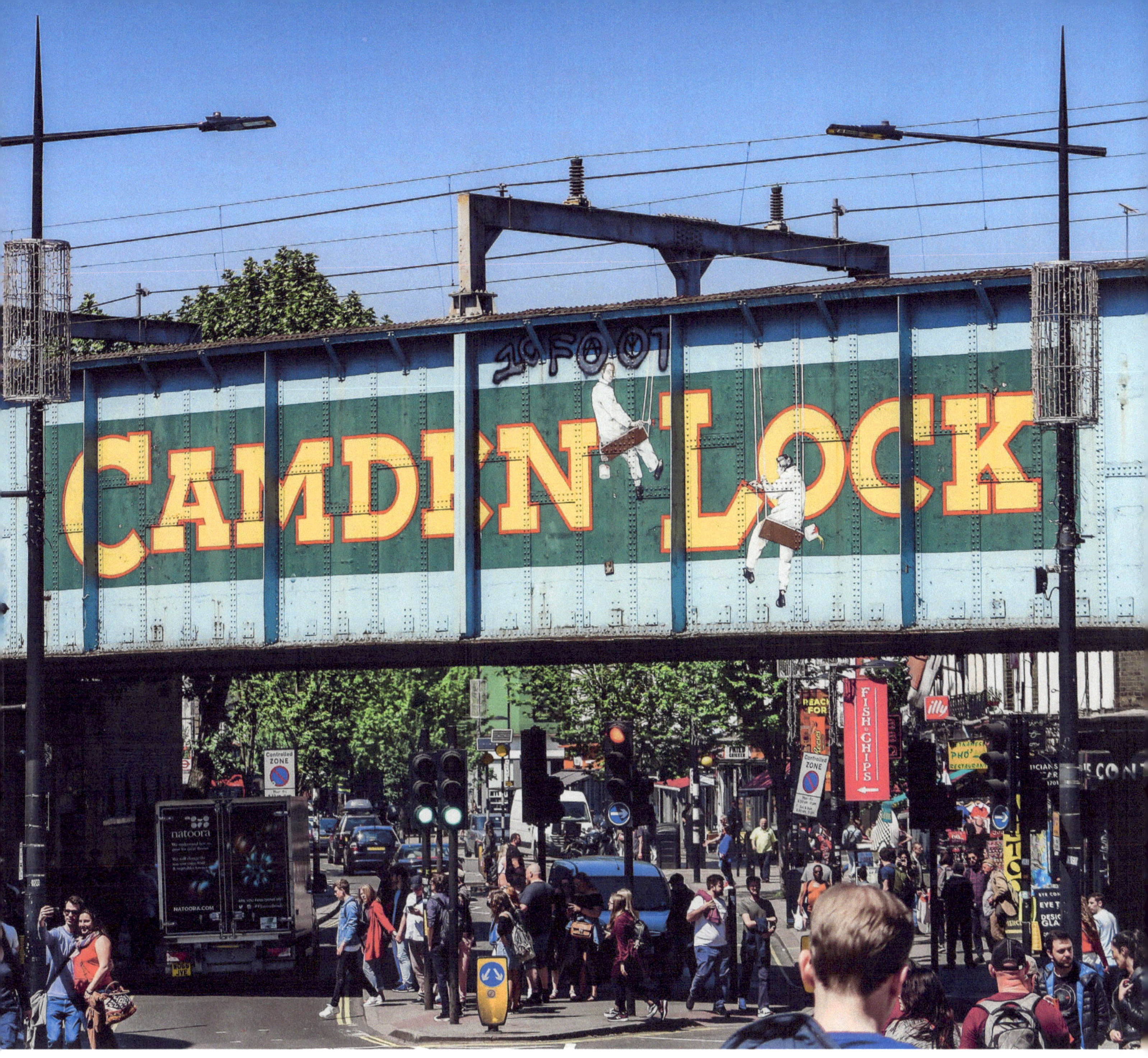

Photo by ZCK

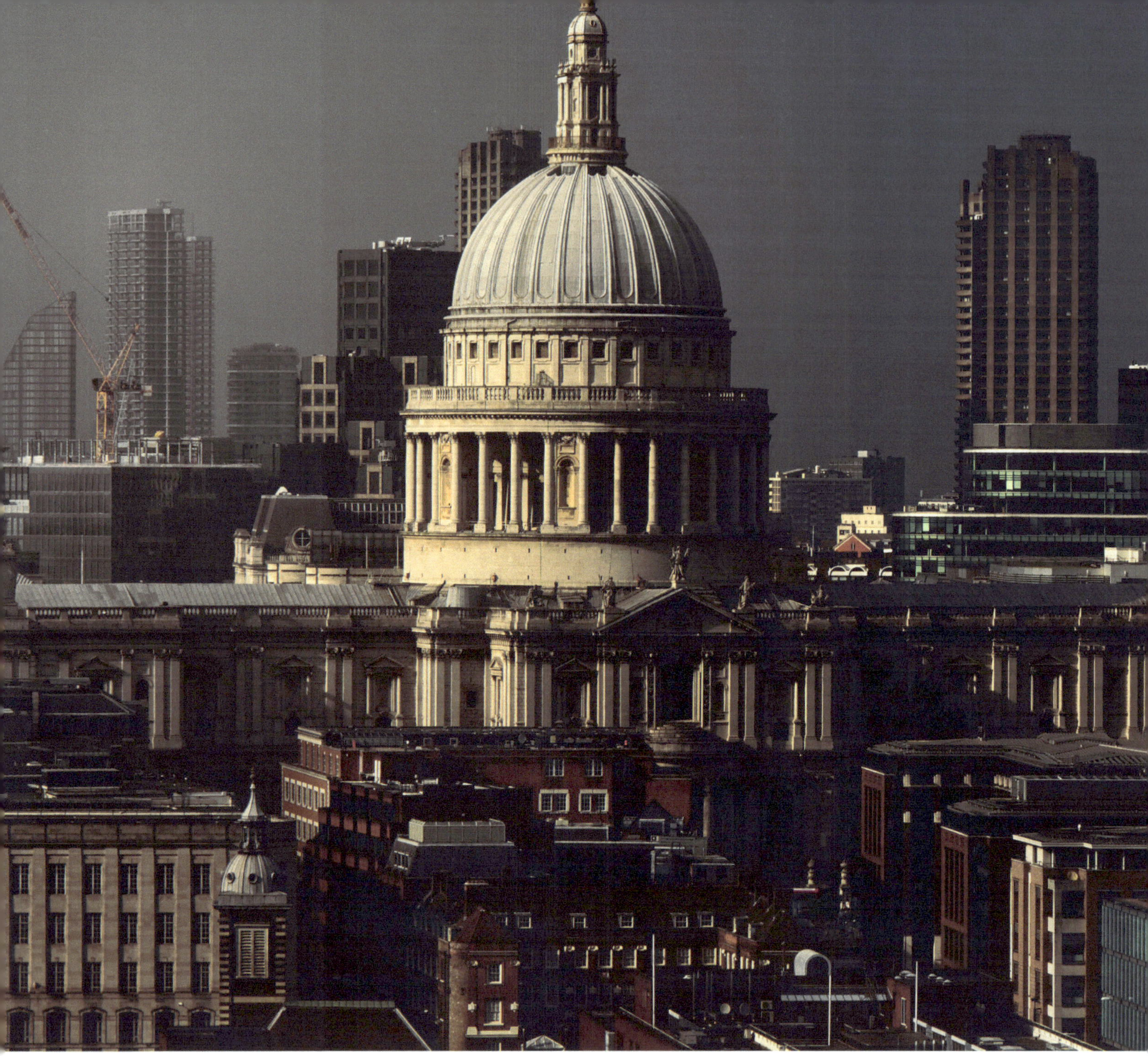

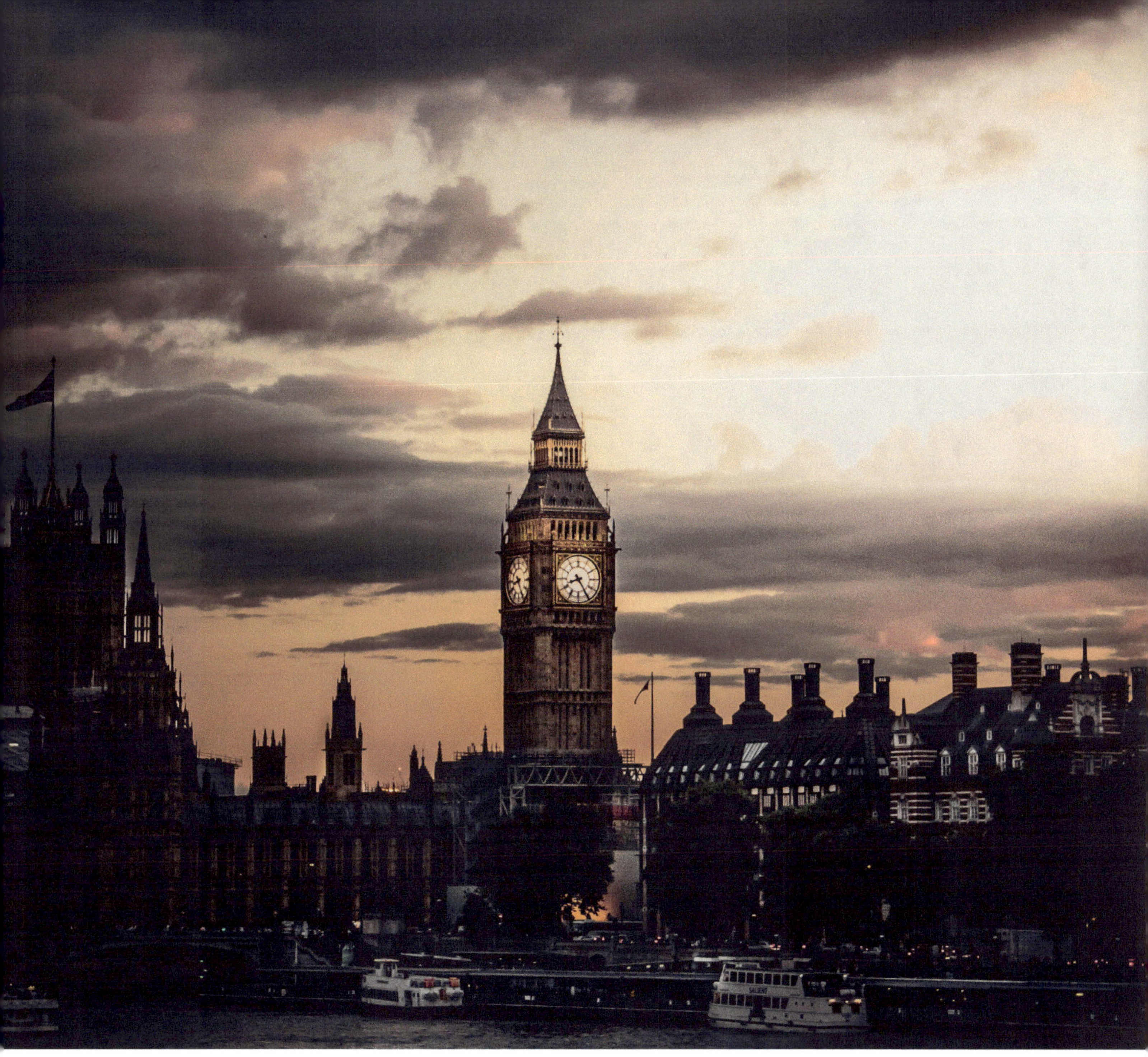

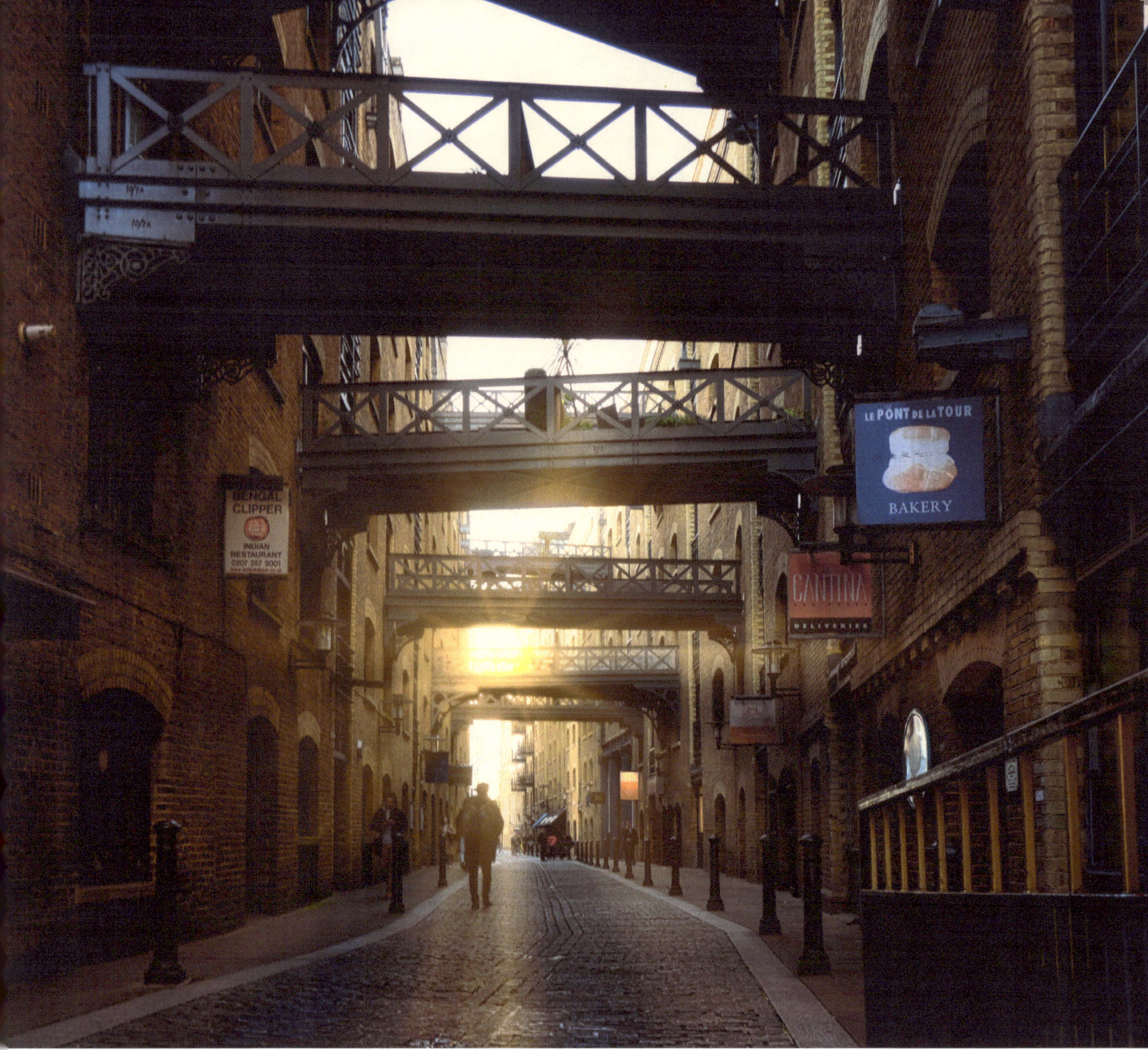

Photo by Mark Higham

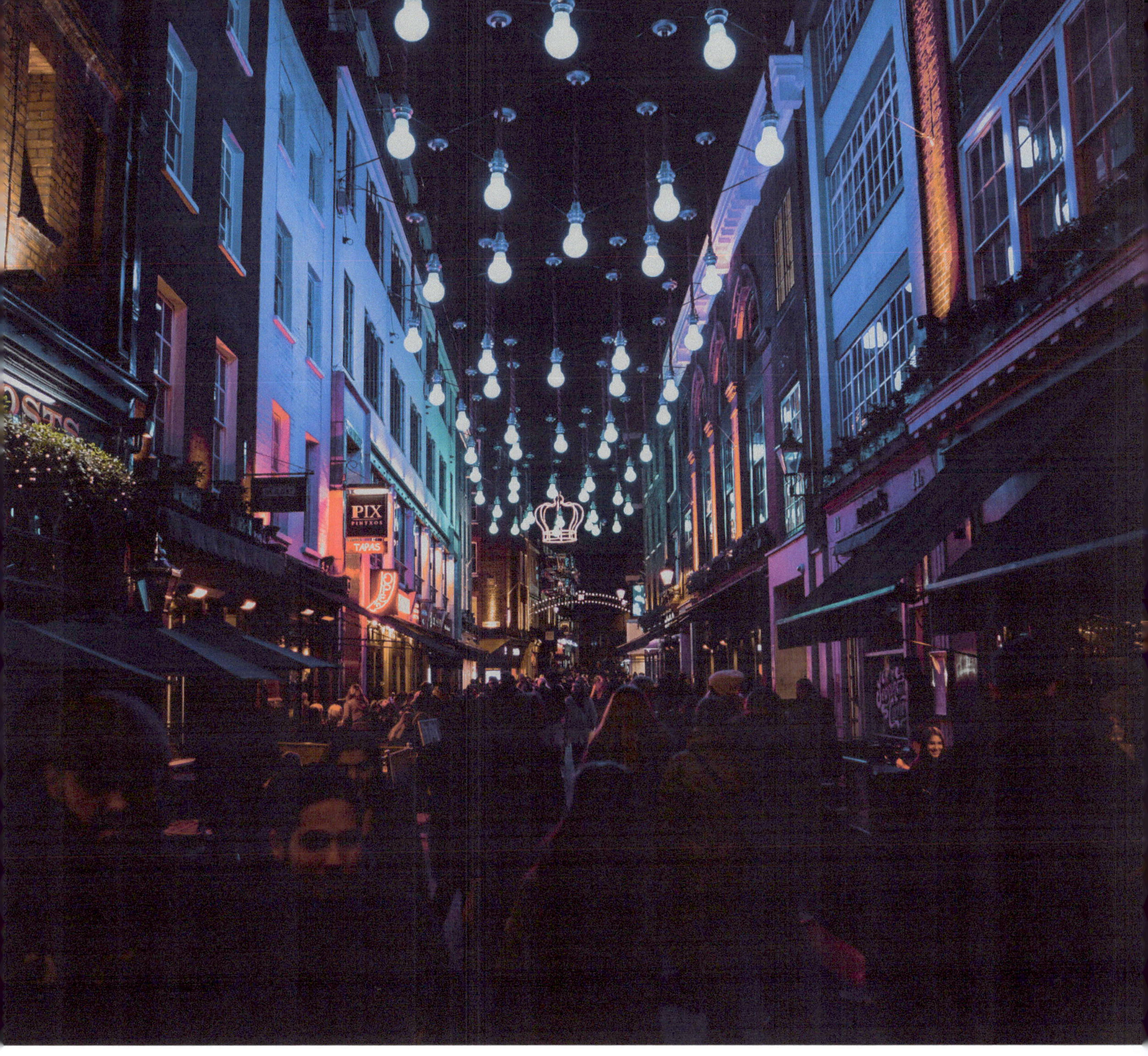

Photo by Marcel Heil

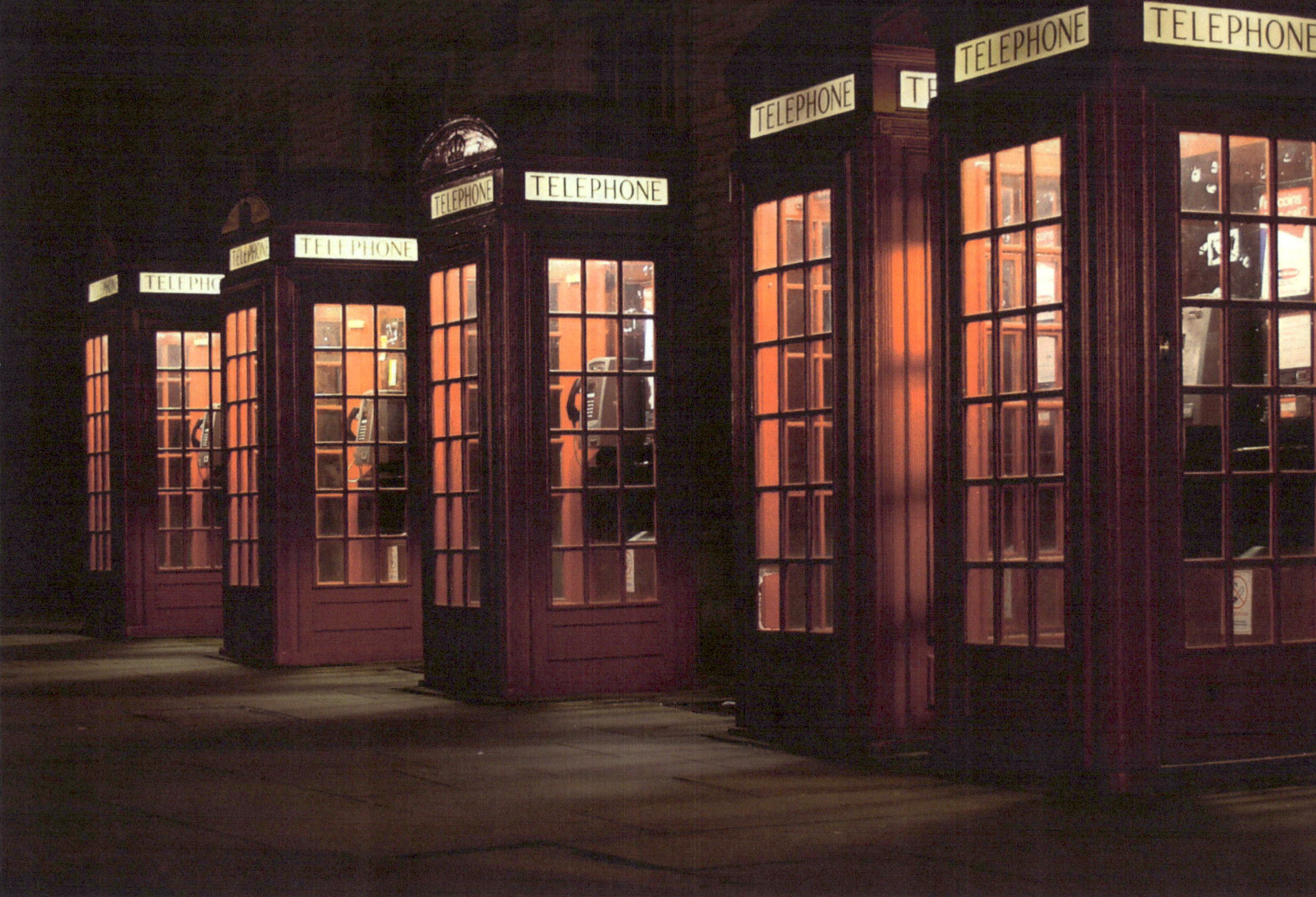

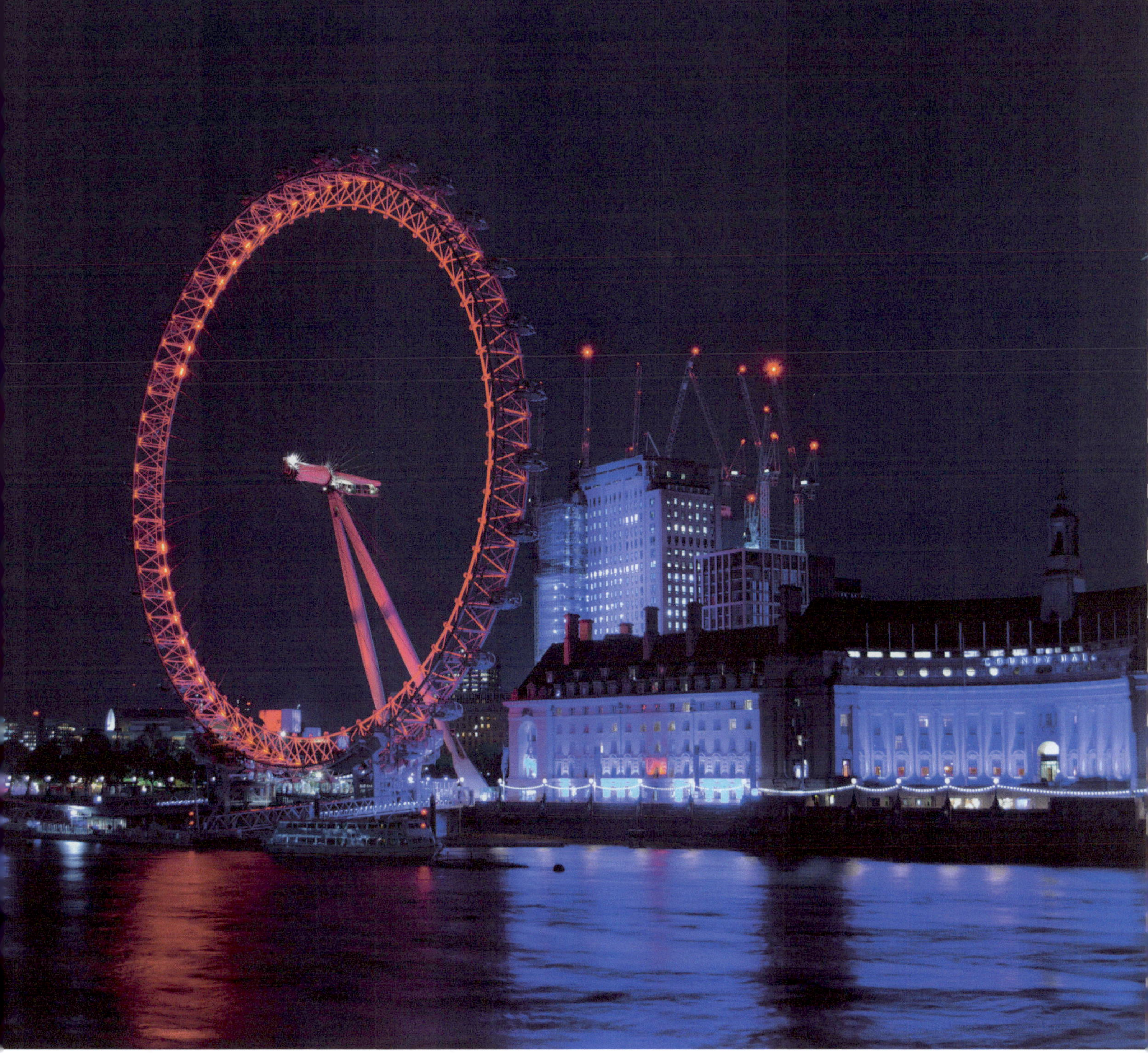

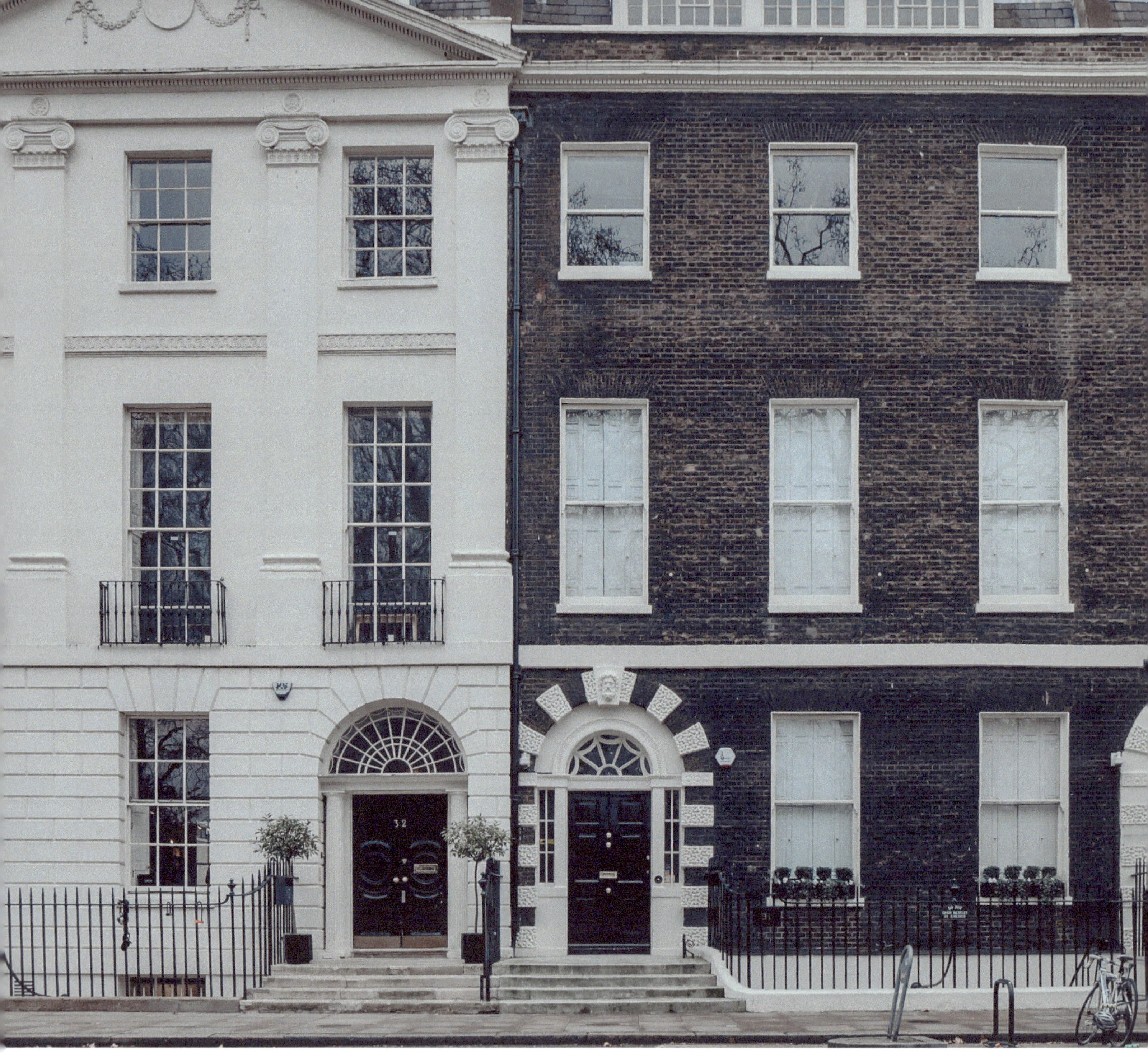

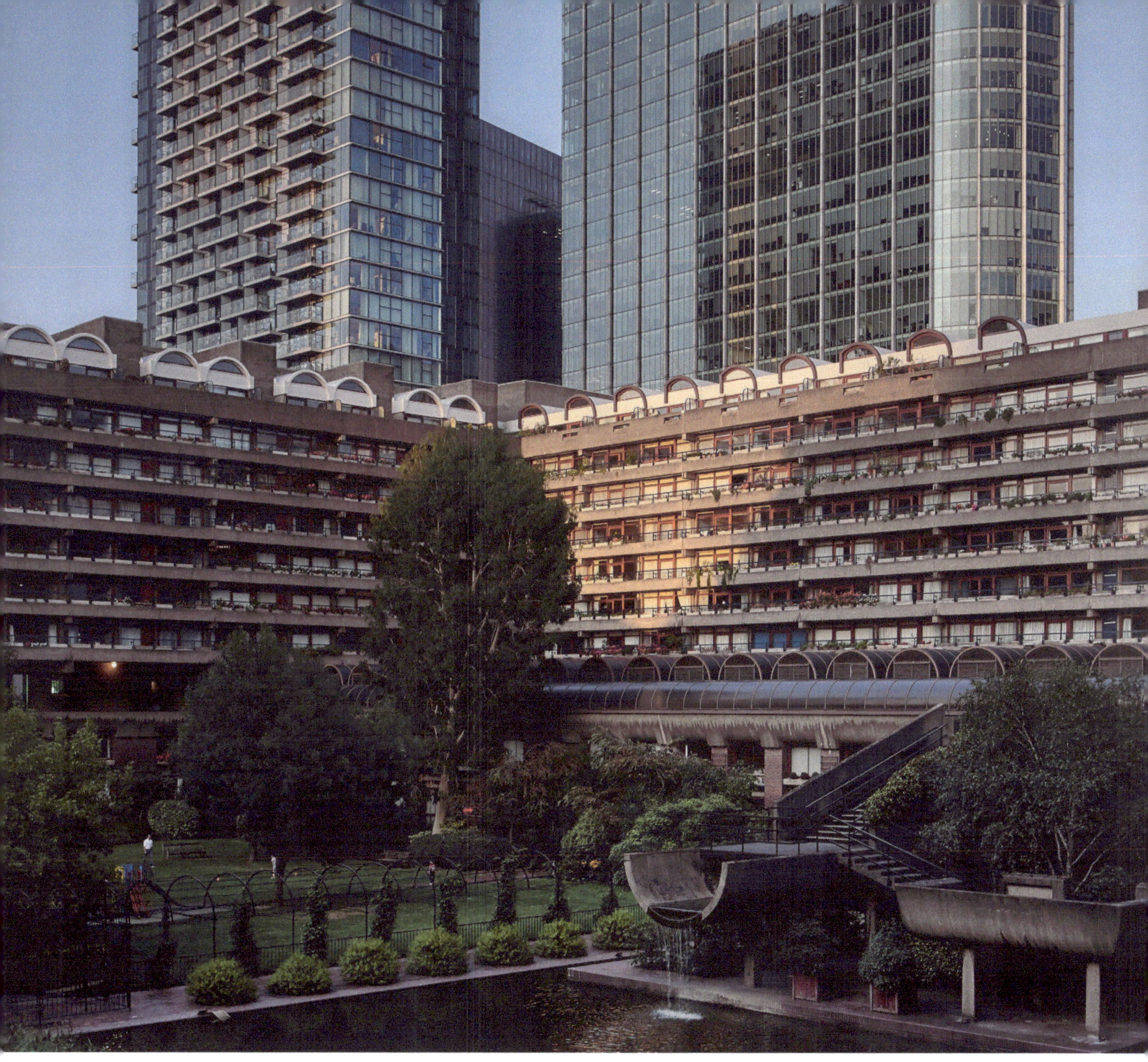

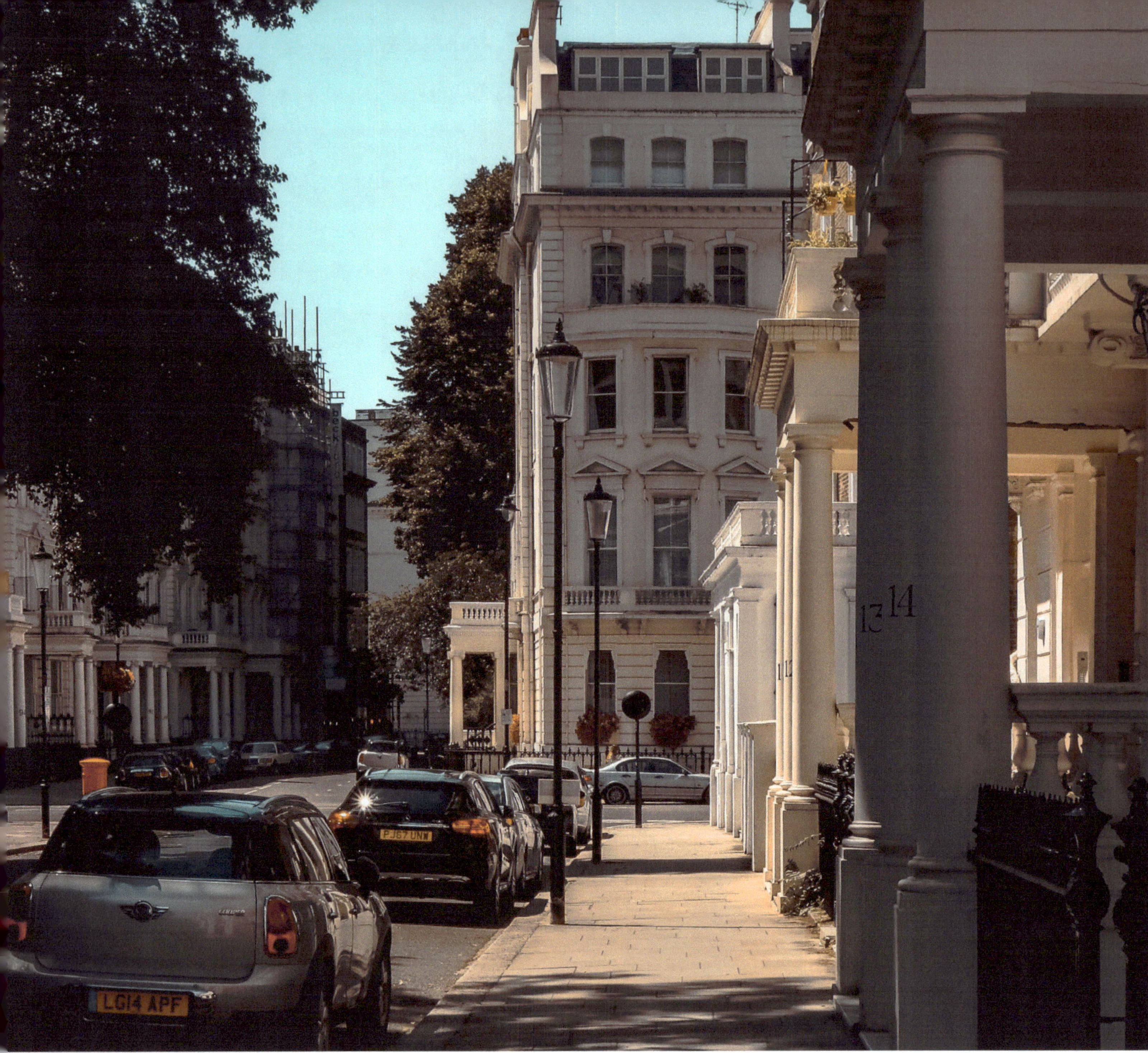

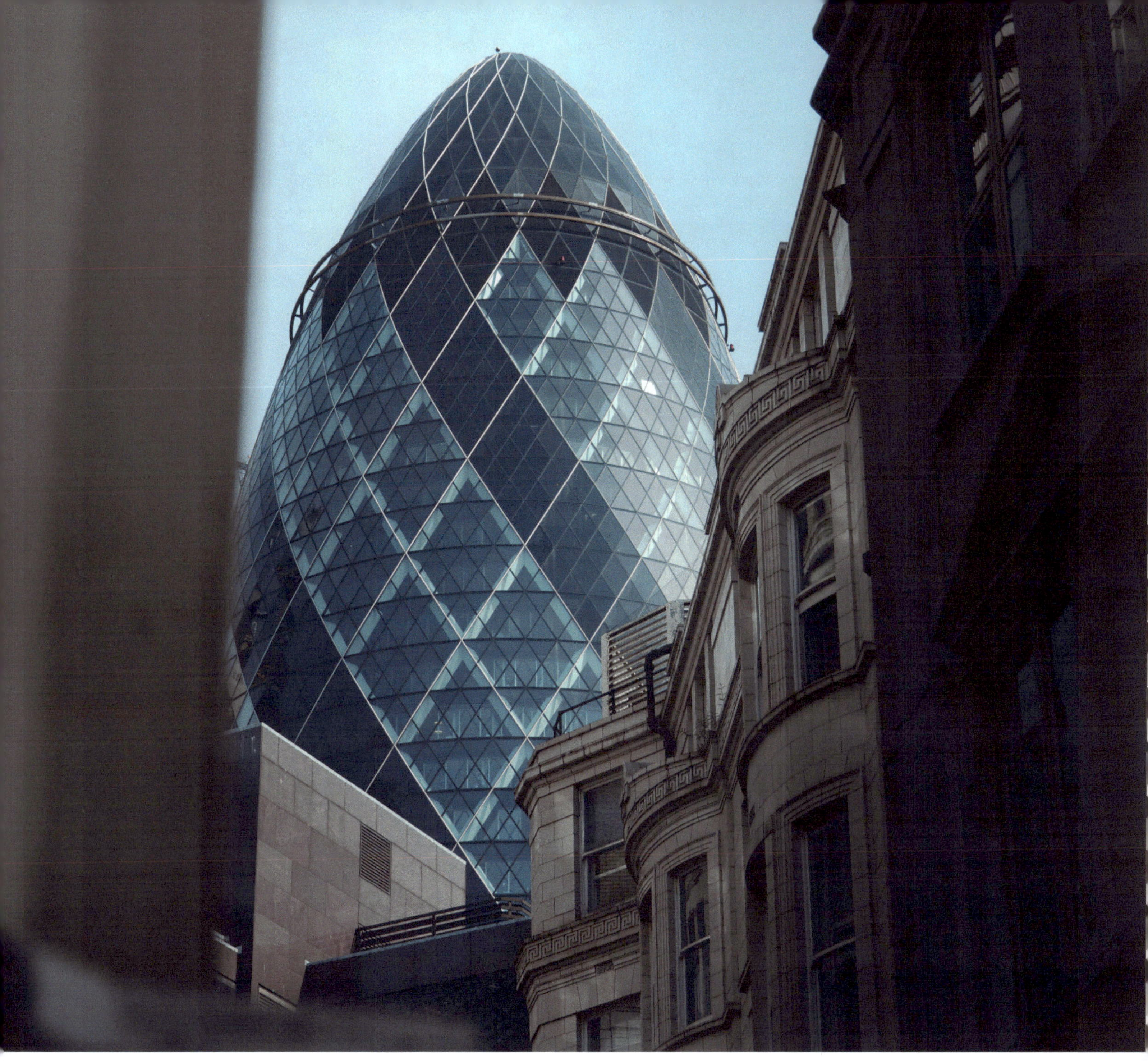

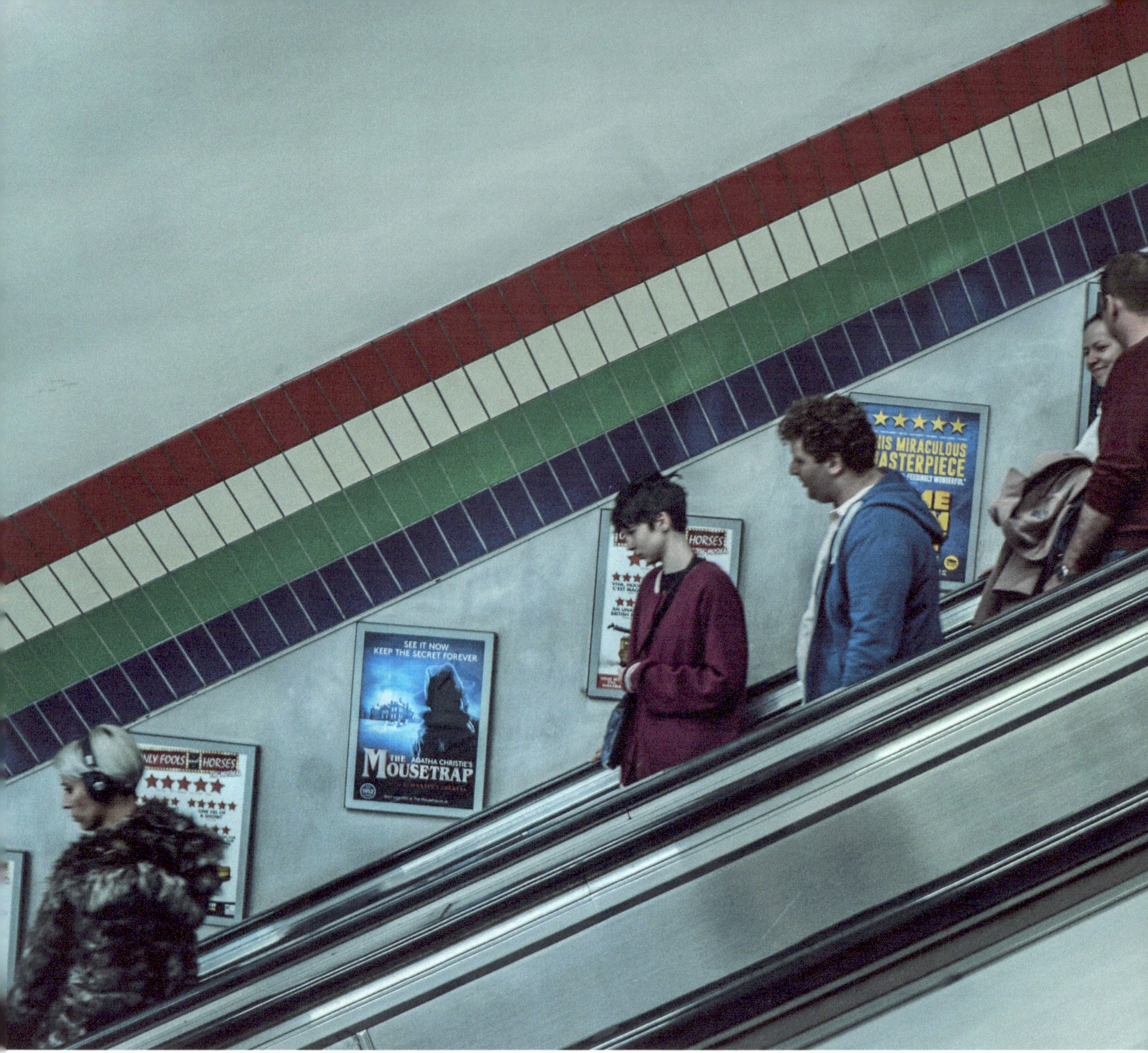

Photo by Mikel Parera

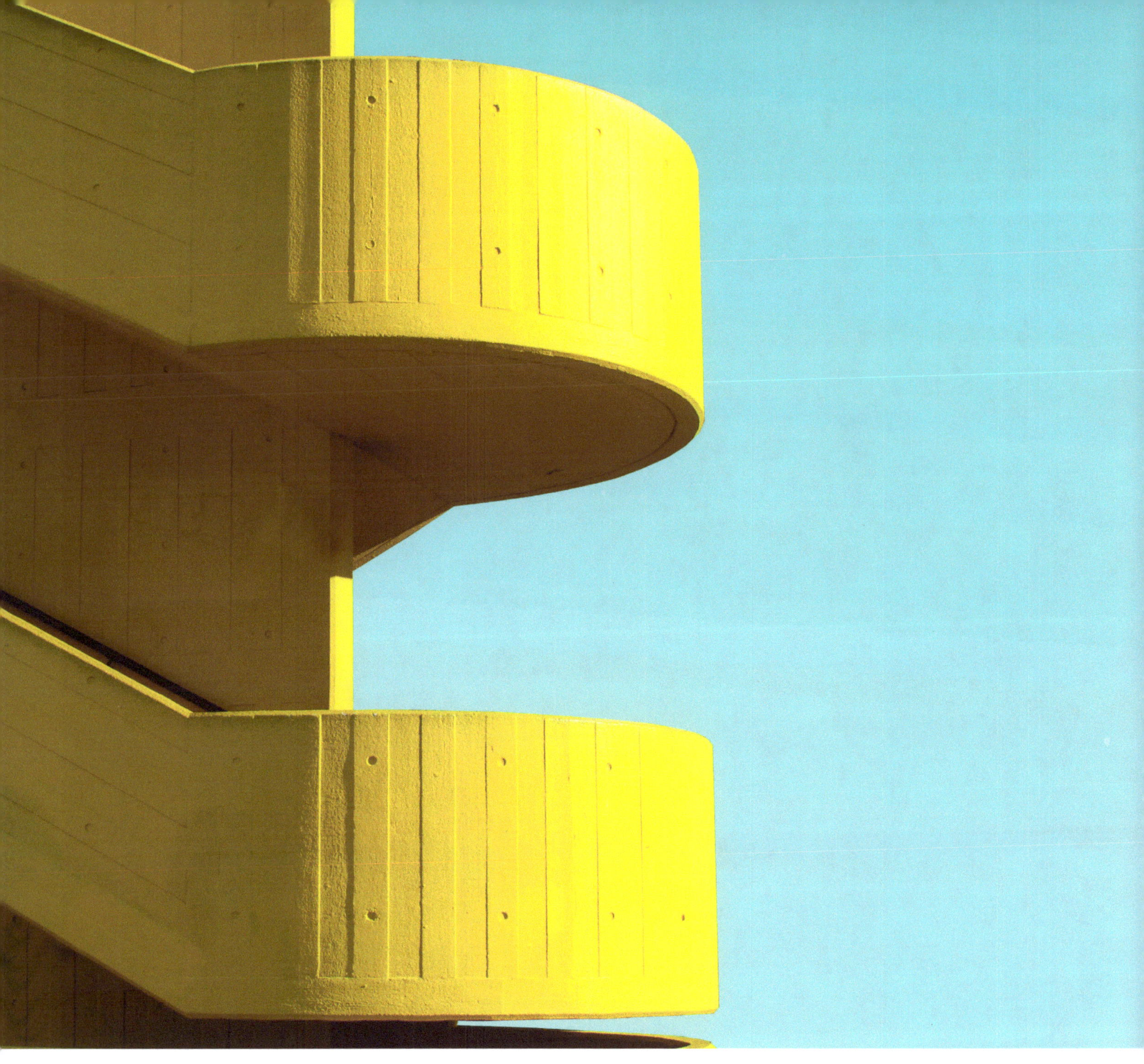

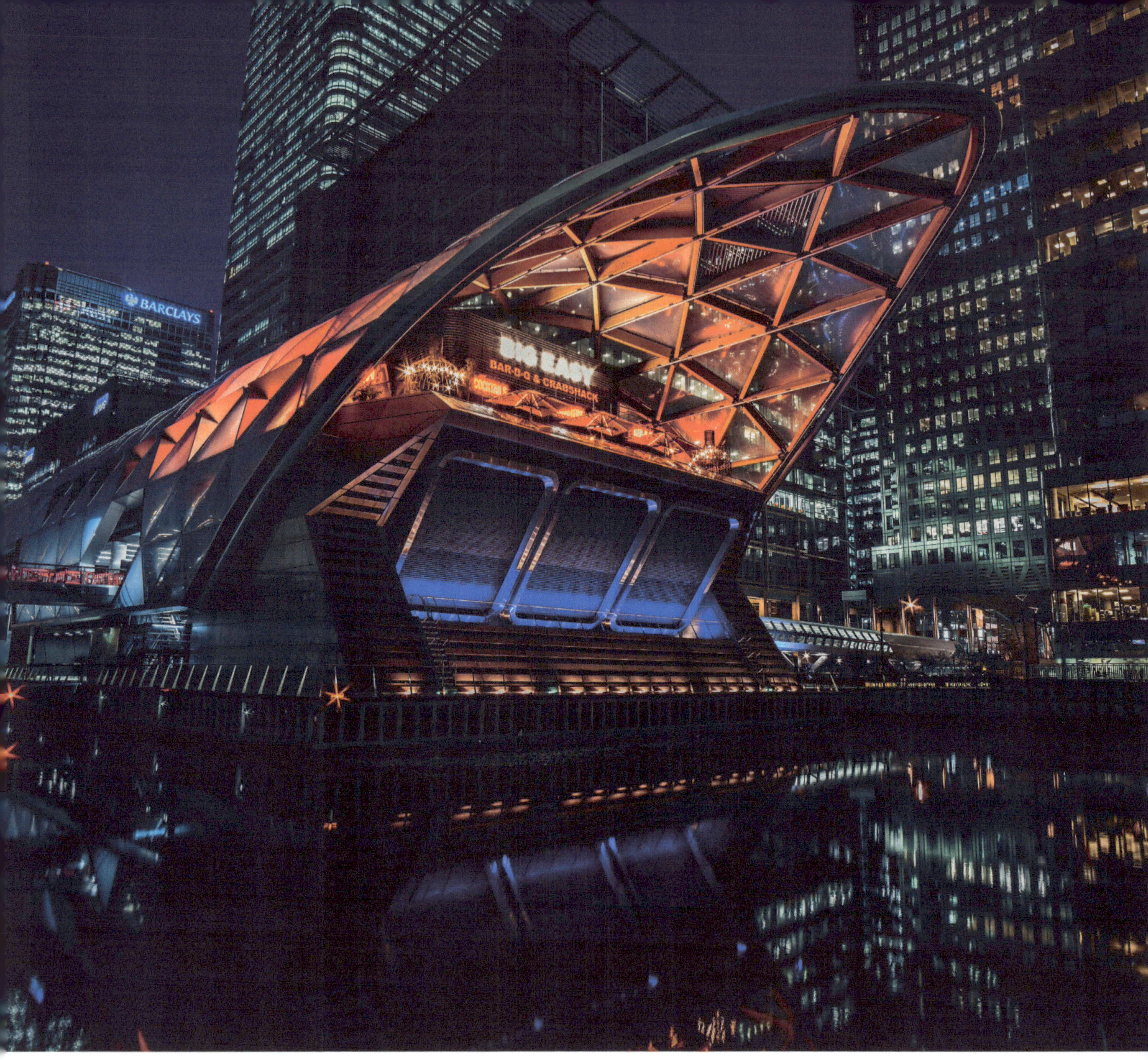

Photo by Myke Simon

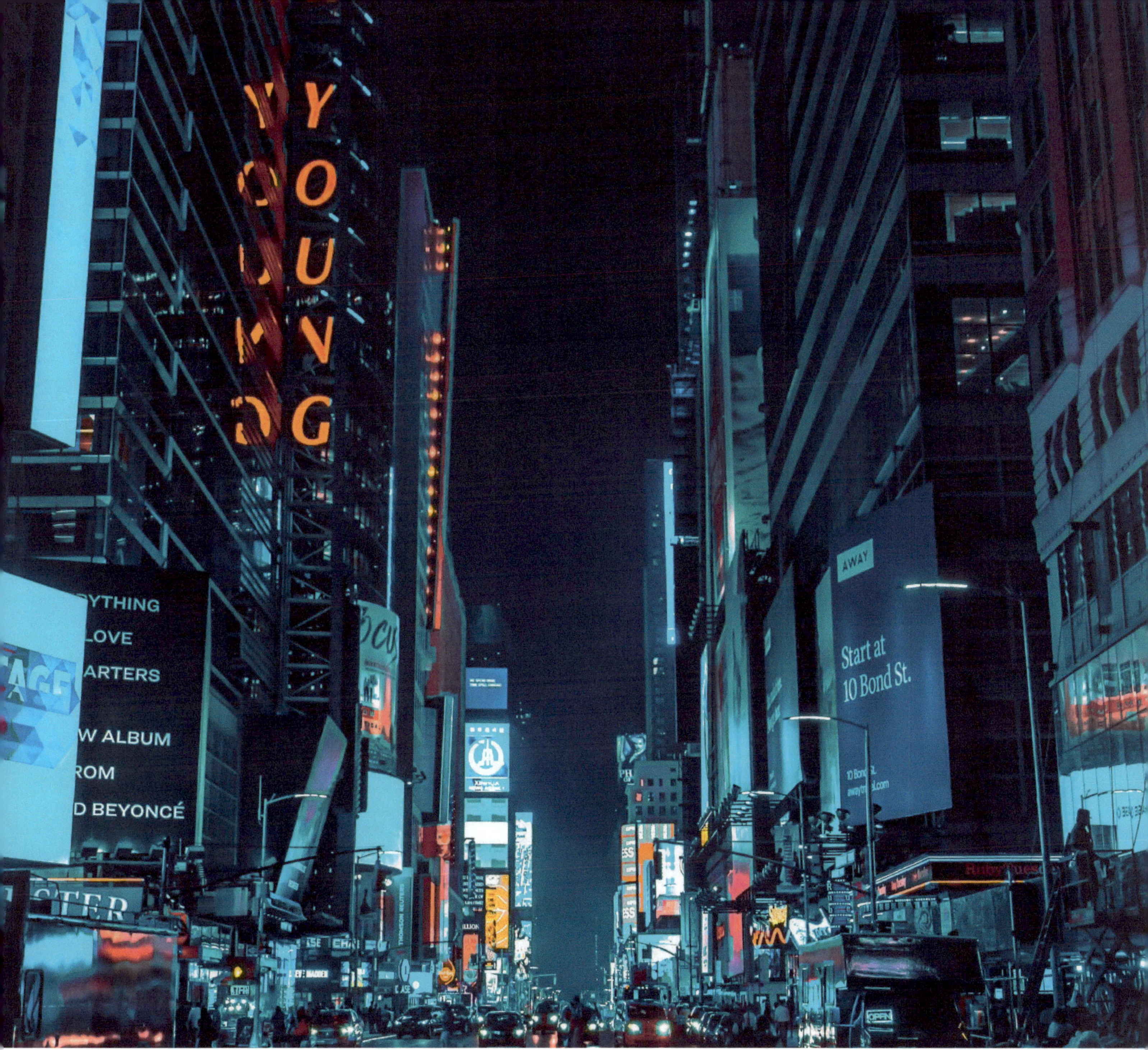

YOUNG
YOUNG
YTHING
LOVE
ARTERS
W ALBUM
ROM
D BEYONCÉ
AWAY
Start at
10 Bond St.

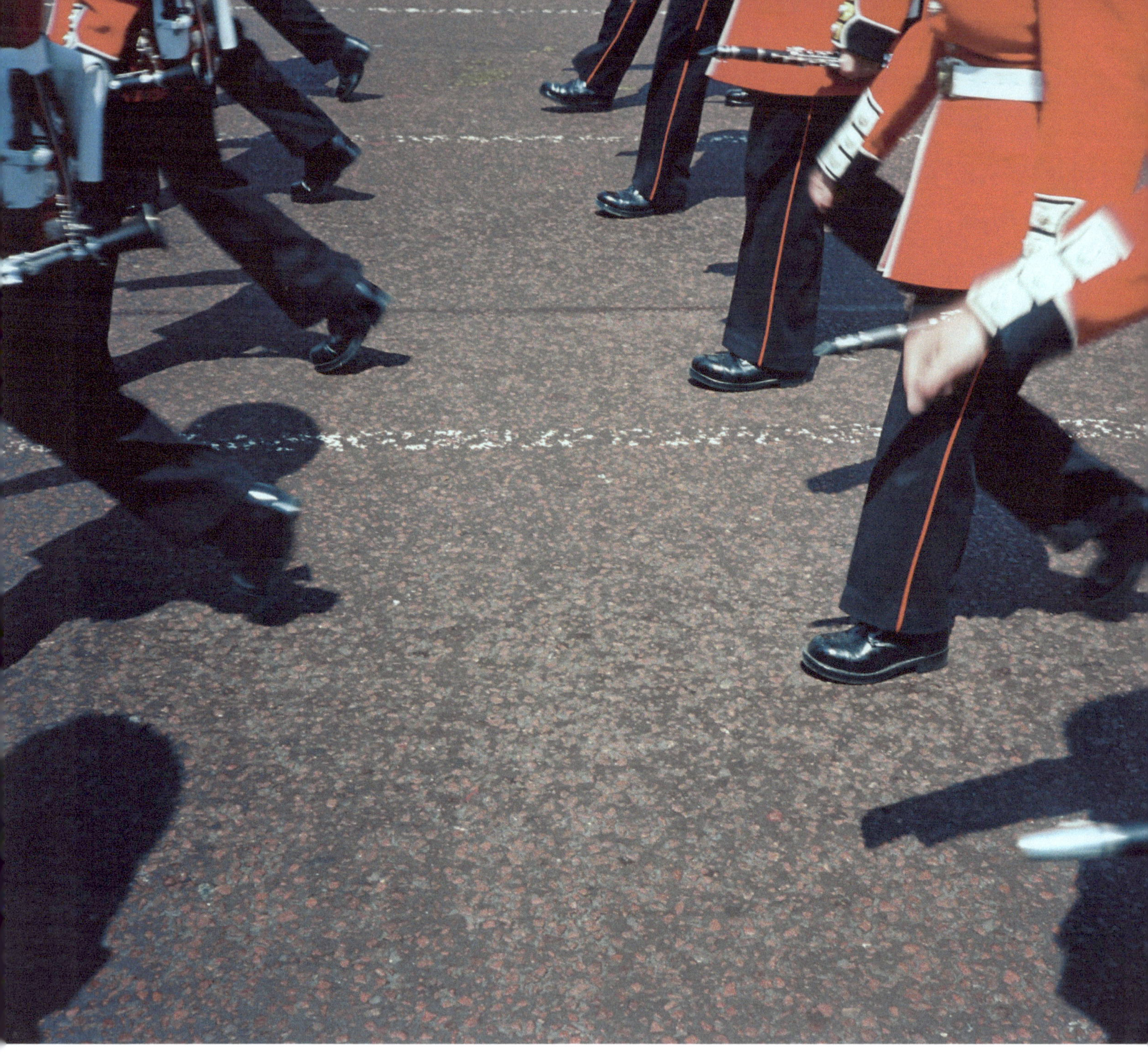

Photo by Nick Page

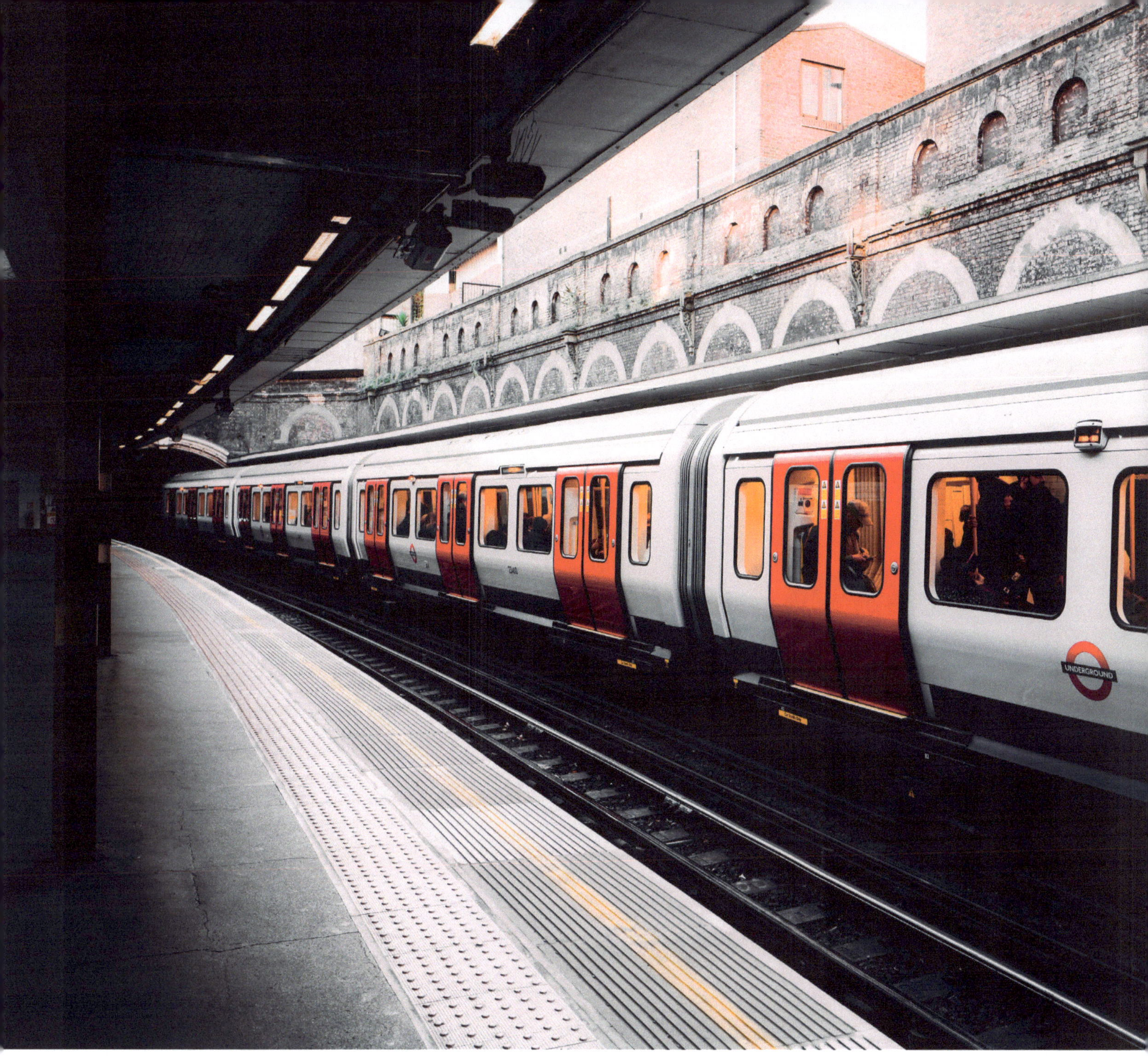

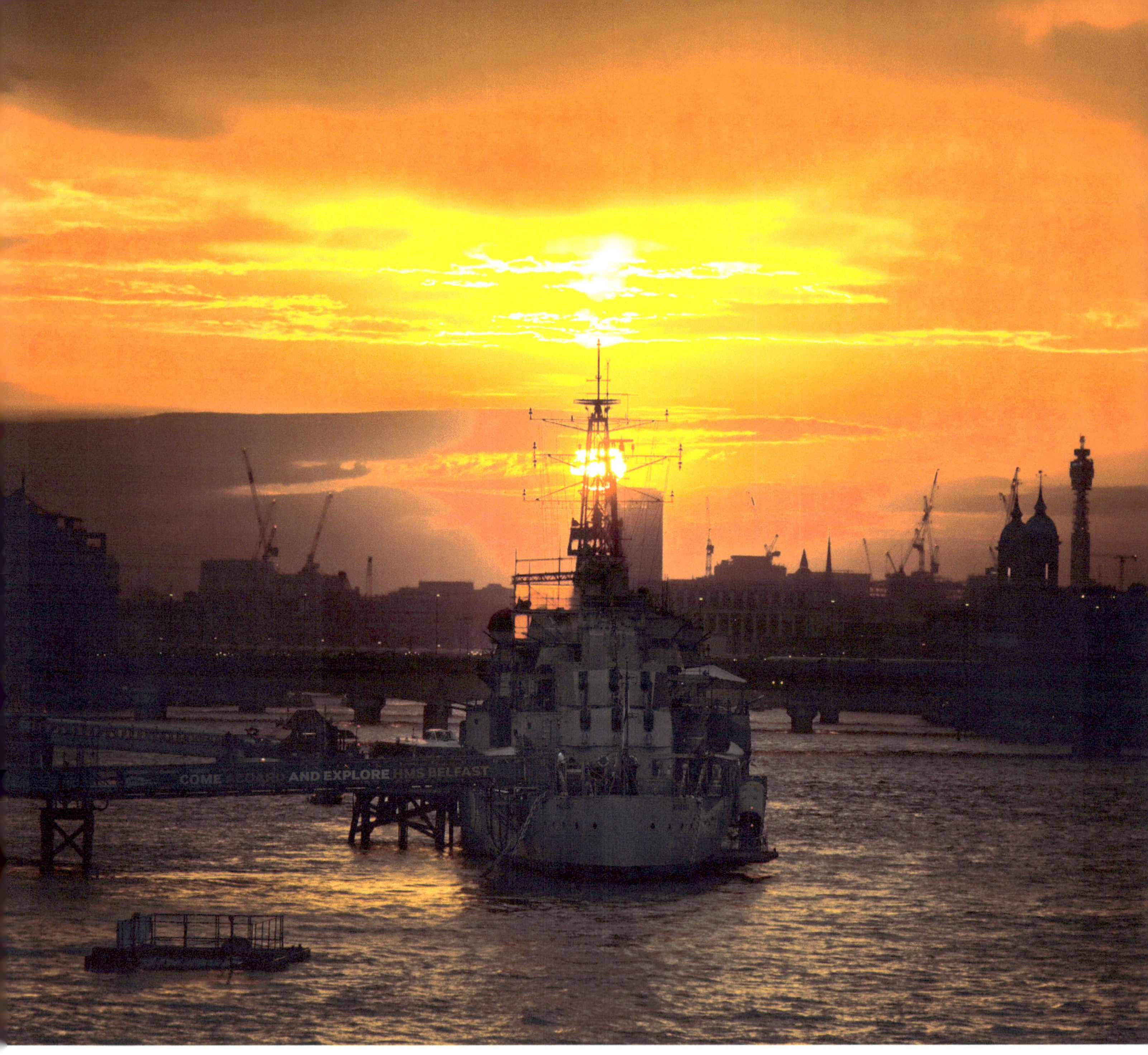

Photo by Roman Fox

Other books in the City Porn Series:

Berlin
London
Los Angeles
New York
Paris